ARCHAEOLOGICAL PERSPECTIVES ON ETHNICITY IN AMERICA

Afro-American and Asian American
Culture History

ARCHAEOLOGICAL PERSPECTIVES ON ETHNICITY IN AMERICA

Afro-American and Asian American
Culture History

EDITED BY
Robert L. Schuyler

Baywood Publishing Company, Inc.

Copyright © 1980 by Baywood Publishing Company, Inc., Farmingdale, New York. All rights reserved.

Printed in the United States of America

International Standard Book Number 0-89503-018-7
Library of Congress Catalog Card Number 79-91229

Library of Congress Cataloging in Publication Data
   Main entry under title:

   Archaeological perspectives on ethnicity in America.

   (Baywood monographs in archaeology ; 1)
   Includes bibliographies.
   1. Afro-Americans—Antiquities—Addresses, essays, lectures. 2. Chinese Americans—Antiquities—Addresses, essays, lectures. 3. United States—Antiquities—Addresses, essays, lectures. I. Schuyler, Robert L., 1947- II. Series.
E185.A72   973'.04'951   79-91229
ISBN 0-89503-018-7

ARCHAEOLOGICAL PERSPECTIVES ON ETHNICITY IN AMERICA

Afro-American and Asian American
Culture History

Preface

Traditionally the subject matter of American archaeology has been limited to the American Indian and major European cultures. Prehistorians have studied Native American prehistory, with a secondary emphasis on the contact periods, in such detail that we now have an outline of human occupation of the New World from almost 20,000 years ago. Historical archaeologists, in turn, have excavated enough Anglo-American, French and Hispanic sites to make major contributions to American history. Ethnic minorities, who were also a significant part of the stream of history in the Western Hemisphere have, however, been neglected. Even with those groups, such as Indians and Hispanics, that were accepted topics of study, such research halted when they were transformed into ethnic minorities within a national structure.

Now a number of scholars have widened research horizons to include cultural groups so frequently cut out of documentary history. Work has started on sites left by several ethnic minorities in the United States resulting in encouraging discoveries but equally perplexing methodological problems. Two of the most critical problems are those of defining ethnicity and recognizing it in the archaeological record. An implicit definition of "ethnic minority" found in this volume equates such a position with incorporation into a dominant national culture. Yet minorities delineated by ethnicity as well as class are also found in traditional societies that predate the rise of nation states. Even the prehistoric city of Teotihuacan in Mexico may have had an Oaxacan minority within its urban neighborhoods. More to the point, there were numerous subgroupings within traditional empires, including Spanish America. There is the possibility of studying ethnicity within the Spanish borderlands but, except for a few projects at urban sites like St. Augustine, this has not really been attempted. Hispanic, or for that matter colonial French or early English, sites are therefore not included in this volume. Only distinct cases of subcultures being incorporated into Anglo-American society are surveyed. Certainly there is an evolutionary factor involved beyond the simple vicissitudes of archaeological fieldwork. Ethnicity has little meaning until complex structures arose based on political domination. At the same time it is not clear whether traditional civilizations were more or less inclined to manipulate ethnicity as an organizational tool as compared to industrial societies. Much of our view of ethnicity may arise from a melting-pot mythology which is a screen for its very antithesis—not a uniform, open national culture but a specific ethnic group controlling the system by suppressing many others. Even within Anglo-American culture the situation is complex. Mormons, for example, might be defined as an ethnic minority between 1830 and 1847, assuming that status again only after 1880. In contrast, during their social, and to some degree political, independence in the Great Basin between 1847 and 1880 (or 1870) they might be classified as a society separate from the mainstream of American history and outside of the national structure.

The archaeology of ethnic minorities does not reveal the spectacular remains of a dominant civilization. Its data contain many truths that will prove unpalatable to both the national mythology and the victims of that mythology. It is, at the same time, not the archaeology of failure. Nor are the common remains it studies of any less interest from an anthropological perspective. Rather it evidences *successful* adaptation and survival. And this very survival creates the second major research problem faced by investigators. Was survival based on the preservation or invention of distinct cultural patterns in language, social structure, economic organization and belief; patterns which would have clearly defined correlates in material culture? Or were the adaptations much broader involving overpowering economic factors resulting in a general culture of poverty with class rather than ethnic boundaries? Is ethnicity, especially the ethnicity of minorities, recognizable in the archaeological record? If so, in what different settings does it evolve, expand, contract or disappear through extinction or assimilation? Or does ethnicity persevere almost indefinitely by radically altering its relationship to the dominant culture? These questions have no easy answers even when social anthropologists are asking them in the present. In the archaeological realm, although there are some encouraging indications, the final answers are certainly in the future awaiting the results of many more excavations and artifact analyses.

Archaeologists, nevertheless, are dealing with these questions in regard to several cultural groups two of which—Black Americans and Asian Americans—have received meaningful attention.

Archaeological Perspectives on Ethnicity in America is the first synthesis of these projects, many unpublished or on-going. It introduces the reader to the exciting prospect of obtaining an independent source of data on minorities separate from written records that were in the main produced by a ruling majority. More replete images of slavery, free Black settlements in the North, Chinese railroad and mining camps, and "China Towns" are being reconstructed. Insights into diet, social relations, degrees of acculturation and basic economic patterns are emerging.

Although almost all the papers in this volume are preliminary or end with tentative conclusions, they do herald the emergence of an entirely new topic in archaeological research in America. A topic of interest to both the profession and the public.

Contents

Preface vii

Part One Introduction 1
Afro-American
Culture History
1 / Race and Class on Antebellum
Plantations
John Solomon Otto 3

2 / Looking for the "Afro" in
Colono-Indian Pottery
Leland Ferguson 14

3 / Archaeological Visiblity of Afro-
American Culture: An Example
from Black Lucy's Garden, Andover,
Massachusetts
Vernon G. Baker 29

4 / Weeksville: The Archaeology of
A Black Urban Community
Sarah T. Bridges and Bert Salwen 38

5 / Sandy Ground: Archaeology of
A 19th Century Oystering Village
Robert L. Schuyler 48

6 / Skunk Hollow: A Preliminary Statement
on Archaeological Investigations at a
19th Century Black Community
Joan H. Geismar 60

7 / The African Meeting House: The Center
for the 19th Century Afro-American
Community in Boston
Beth Anne Bower and Byron Rushing 69

8 / Archaeology of Black American Culture:
An Annotated Bibliography
Geoffrey M. Gyrisco and Bert Salwen 76

Part Two
Asian American Culture History

Introduction 87

9 / Food and Fantasy: Material Culture of the Chinese in California and the West, Circa 1850-1900
William S. Evans, Jr. 89

10 / The West Coast Chinese and Opium Smoking
Patricia A. Etter 97

11 / The Archaeology of 19th Century Chinese Subsistence at the Lower China Store, Madera County, California
Paul E. Langenwalter, II 102

12 / The Chinese on Main Street
Roberta S. Greenwood 113

13 / Archaeology of Asian American Culture: An Annotated Bibliography
Robert L. Schuyler 124

Part Three
Archaeology and Ethnicity

14 / Approaches to Ethnic Identification in Historical Archaeology
Marsha C. S. Kelly and Roger E. Kelly 133

Contributors 145

PART ONE
Afro-American Culture History

Introduction

Black Americans, unlike many other ethnic groups, have been part of American history since its inception. They have also experienced situations unparalleled by other groups ranging from chattel slavery to demographic domination of a number of regions in the South. The seven chapters in this section, and a few previously published works (Deetz 1977; Handler and Lange 1978), are concerned with several interconnected archaeological themes. One of the most fascinating but difficult is the survival of Africanisms in material culture. Two others, that strongly influence the first, are rural-urban relationships and a closed versus an open association with general American society.

African survivals actually involve a number of overlapping possibilities that range from direct African diffusion, that survived the middle passage, through traits specific only to Afro-Americans, irrespective of their ultimate origins, to a general, non-ethnic culture of poverty.

Some of the first field projects in Afro-American archaeology were initiated by Charles Fairbanks and his colleagues and students at the University of Florida. Although initially Africanisms were not detected it has been plantation sites in Barbados and on the Sea Islands off Georgia that now most clearly reveal possible African or at least distinct Afro-American traits. Indeed in the Barbados study there are isolated African elements in the earliest materials although they gradually phase out with the passage of time.

In the more open system of the Northeast and Post-Bellum South the situation is much more indistinct. Many sites, especially rural settlements, are being found not to be solely Black inhabited but simultaneously or alternately Black-White occupied. There is an important lesson involved (even if the archaeologist would prefer a clear cut situation) — segregation itself was only an ideal cultural pattern lacking a total correlation with day to day human behavior. Although some specific artifact patterns and faunal remains are associated with Afro-American communities, archaeologists must be extremely cautious at this stage of research. Are such traits ethnically peculiar or found across all impoverished groups in a society?

Archaeological images of the Afro-American past such as Deetz (1977) has proffered for Parting Ways, an 18-19th century settlement of Black Revolutionary War veterans near Plymouth, Massachusetts, are very debatable. Excavators must not be overenthusiastic in their search for Africanisms even if such finds might please contemporary minority members. Cultures are adaptive systems and do not exist or survive in historical vacuums. One of the primary contributions of Afro-American archaeology may not be evidence for perseverance but rather evidence of human ability to constantly alter or even totally invent new cultural patterns.

Bibliography

Deetz, James
    1977   Parting Ways. Chapter 7 in *In Small Things Forgotten, the Archaeology of Early American Life*. Garden City, New York: Anchor Press/Doubleday.

Handler, Jerome and Frederick W. Lange
    1978   *Plantation Slavery In Barbados*. Cambridge, Massachusetts: Harvard University Press.

CHAPTER 1

Race and Class on Antebellum Plantations

JOHN SOLOMON OTTO

For several decades, archaeologists who have excavated sites in complex societies have confronted the same problem: How are status differences reflected in the archaeological remains? Traditionally archaeologists have routinely inferred the status of site inhabitants from the quality and quantity of archaeological evidence, even though the true status of the inhabitants was unknown (e.g., Trigger in Chang 1968). Many archaeologists have assumed that there was a perfect correlation between the archeaological remains they found and the status of the former site inhabitants. They assumed that high status was always associated with higher quality and quantities of housing, possessions, and foods; in turn, they assumed that low status was always associated with lower quality and quantities of material rewards.

In complex societies, however, there are a great variety of status differences which may produce patterning in the archaeological record. In addition to age and sex differences, there are racial, ethnic, linguistic, occupational, legal, and political differences. These various status positions are ranked in hierarchies and have differing access to symbolic and material rewards. These rewards include power or the legal right to coerce others; psychic rewards such as prestige, dignity, security, and a sense of independence, and property or access to material wealth and labor (Tumin 1967: 39-46; Warner in Tumin 1970: 233, 241). Evidence of these symbolic and material rewards may be difficult to recover at archaeological sites. The symbolic rewards such as power and prestige, which may have been of equal or greater concern to site inhabitants than material rewards, will be lost or only partially described in the incomplete written record. In turn, since so much of material culture is perishable, material rewards such as housing, possessions, and foods will be only partially preserved in the incomplete written record.

Furthermore, status positions and access to material rewards are not perfectly associated in complex societies (Laumann and others, eds., 1970: 63-65). Frequently, people occupy relatively high status positions which have only symbolic rewards or material rewards that are not commensurate with their standing. Conversely, other people occupy relatively low positions but accumulate material rewards that are not commensurate with their true status. Given this imperfect association between status and material rewards, the material conditions in which former site inhabitants lived may not always reflect their actual status positions. It is even possible that the archaeological remains from many sites will not reflect any status patterning.

In Old South society (1789-1861), for example, access to power, prestige, and material rewards was not perfectly associated with status. Not infrequently, there were similarities in the daily living conditions of many Old South whites and blacks despite differences in racial, legal, and social status. In a classic article, Avery Craven outlined the basic similarities in the housing, food, clothing, daily tasks, and recreation of white yeoman farmers, poorer whites, and black slaves (Craven 1930: 16-18). Though free Southern whites had higher racial and legal status than black slaves, their higher status was not always associated with superior material rewards. In fact, many black slaves may have had better housing, possessions, and foods than some of the poorer whites (Genovese 1974: 24, 63, 533). Consequently, archaeologists who are excavating antebellum Southern sites cannot always accurately infer the status of former site inhabitants from the archaeological remains of their living conditions—the quality and quantity of housing, artifacts, and food remains. Given our present limited knowledge of Old South sites, archaeologists should attempt to identify the true status of former site inhabitants rather than simply inferring status from the archaeological remains.

Fortunately, historical archaeologists usually have an independent set of data—written documents and oral testimony—which can be used to identify the true racial, legal, and social status of the people who occupied the houses, used the artifacts, and ate the foods that appear at antebellum archaeological sites. With documentary controls, correlations can be established between the status of the site inhabitants and the archaeological remains they left behind.

At Old South plantations, for example, the true identity and status of the inhabitants can often be established from documents. Frequently, representatives of the three major social groups of the Old South—white planters, black slaves, and white overseers, who were usually the sons of middle class farmers—could be found living on the same plantation (Wall in Link and Patrick 1965: 177; Bonner in Link and Patrick 1965: 158). After identifying the dwelling sites of the plantation inhabitants, the dwellings and associated features can be dated with documents and artifacts to ensure that the archaeological evidence from the sites dates to the same period in time. With documentary and chronological controls, differences in housing, artifacts, and food remains at plantation dwelling sites can be explained by differences in known status during the same period in time. Since the inhabitants differed in racial and social status, the archaeological evidence can be used to test hypotheses about status differences and their reflection in the archaeological record.

Such a situation existed at Cannon's Point Plantation, St. Simons Island, Georgia (Figure 1), a long-staple cotton plantation where documents attested to the presence of black slaves, white overseers, and a white planter family—the Coupers, who owned Cannon's Point from 1793-1866. The dwelling sites

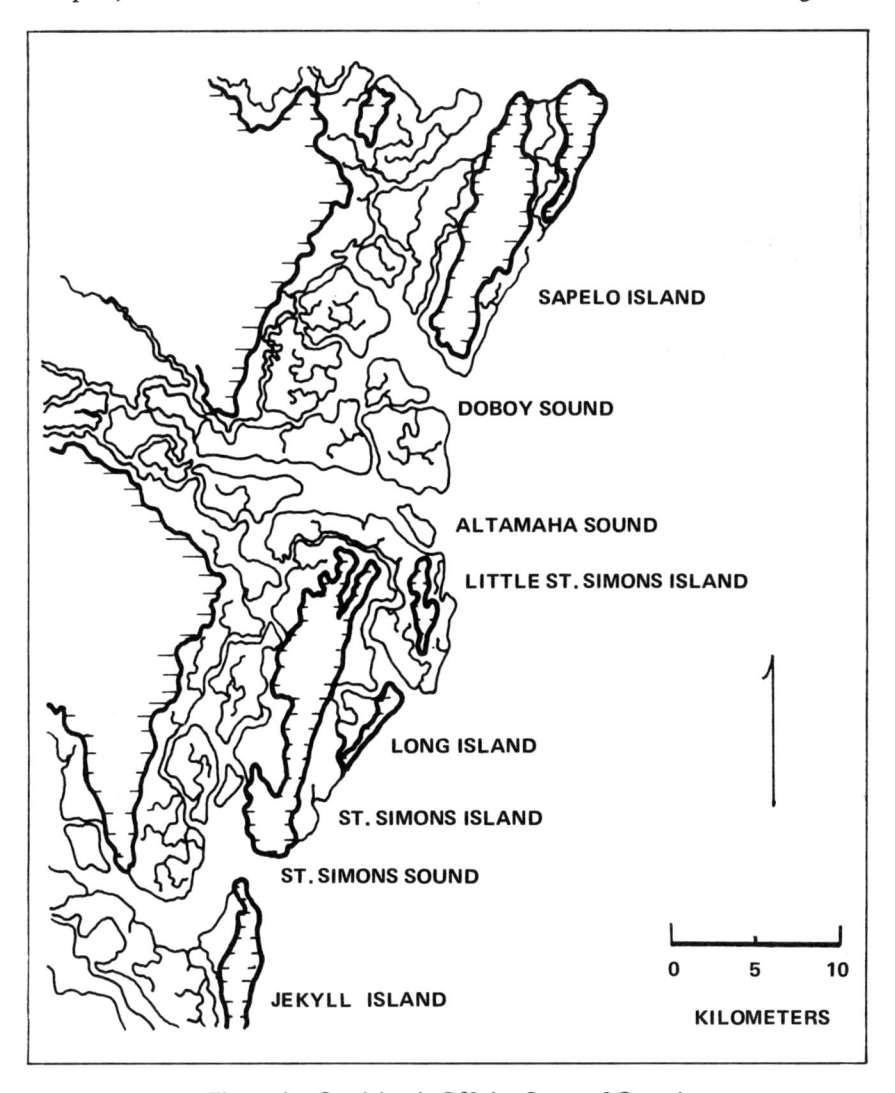

Figure 1. Sea Islands Off the Coast of Georgia

6 / JOHN SOLOMON OTTO

occupied by slaves, overseers, and planters were identified from documents as well as analogies with the settlement patterns of other coastal cotton plantations.

At Cannon's Point, the planter's house was located on the banks of a tidal river, and it was surrounded by the cotton houses and storehouses. The northern set of four single slave cabins was located near the planter's complex; in turn, another set of four duplex slave cabins was located at the southern end of the plantation. The overseers' house was placed in a central location, so the overseers could police both slave quarters. (Figure 2).

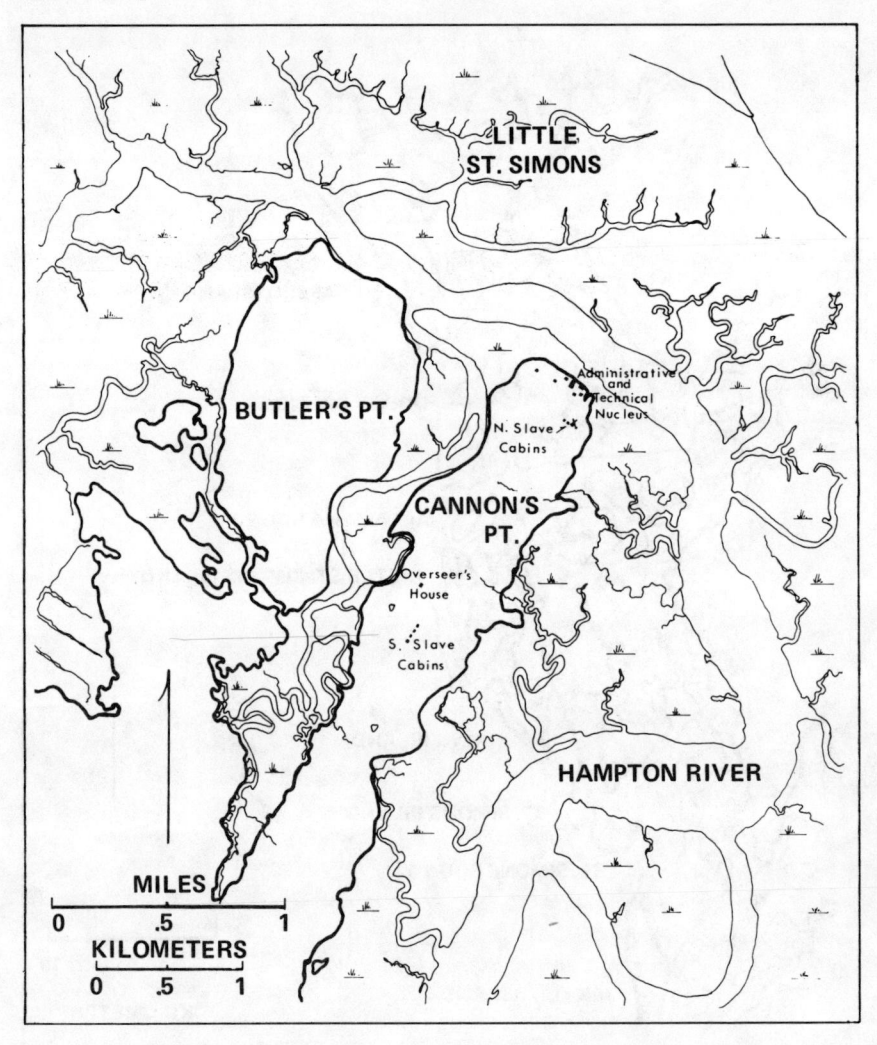

Figure 2. Settlement Pattern of the Cannon's Point Plantation, St. Simons Island, Georgia

These ruined dwellings and the refuse middens in their "backyards" appeared to be relatively undisturbed. As Charles Fairbanks noted in a paper presented at the Society for Historical Archaeology meeting in 1972, the "backyards" of historic sites, especially the refuse disposal areas, contained much of the data that archaeologists needed to test explanatory hypotheses about cultural processes, (Fairbanks MS; Fairbanks 1976: 165). To test our hypotheses about status differences and the archaeological record, the Cannon's Point excavations focused on the refuse areas associated with dwellings once occupied by planters, overseers, and slaves (Fairbanks 1976: 171).

At the planter's site, we mapped the standing ruins, conducted test excavations inside the ruins, and sampled the refuse midden associated with the planter's kitchen. In turn, we cleared and mapped the overseers' house ruins and sampled the associated refuse midden. And at the third slave cabin in the northern slave quarters, we excavated a one room cabin and sampled its associated refuse midden (Figure 2). From documents, we knew the dwellings had been constructed during the antebellum years (US Coast Survey 1869). In addition, the excavations yielded antebellum refuse contexts at all three sites. Three refuse zones in the planter's kitchen midden contained no artifacts whose beginning date of manufacture was later than 1860; the ceramics from these zones provided mean ceramic dates of ca. 1815, 1818, and 1824. Two refuse zones in the overseers' house midden contained only antebellum artifacts; the ceramics in these zones dated to ca. 1821. Finally, a refuse zone in the slave cabin midden, which contained only antebellum artifacts, yielded a mean ceramic date of ca. 1817 (Otto in South 1977: 92, Appendix A).

With chronological controls, it was possible to compare ruins, artifacts, and food remains which dated to the antebellum occupation of the plantation (1793-1861). And with documentary controls, it was possible to establish the true identity and status of the plantation inhabitants. Since status and chronology were held as constants, the differences and similarities in the archaeological remains at all three sites could be explained by differences and similarities in known status (South 1972: 100).

In addition to differing in known status, the Cannon's Point inhabitants are known to have had differing access to the plantation surplus—the cash crops, the food crops, and the livestock produced on the plantation, or their equivalent value in cash. The Couper family who owned and managed their estate monopolized the surplus: they sold crops on the market; they reinvested the profits; or they spent considerable sums on household necessities and luxuries. Although the slaves produced the plantation crops under the supervision of the hired overseers, the slaves and overseers had only limited access to the plantation surplus. In return for their labor, the slaves only received rations of food and textiles, gifts of some household articles, and the use of cabins. In return for long hours of field supervision, the overseers only received the use of a house and yearly incomes ranging from $200 to $400. Using credit on their incomes, the overseers had to buy their own food, clothing, and many of their household utensils (Couper 1826-52; Couper 1839-54; Wolf 1959: 136-138).

The lower status of the slaves and overseers and their limited access to the plantation surplus may have been reflected in the archaeological remains of their housing, possessions, and foods. Nevertheless, the archaeological remains could have reflected several kinds of known status.

First, the people who lived on Cannon's Point Plantation differed in racial and legal status. The inhabitants included free whites as well as black slaves.

Racial/Legal Status

Planters and Overseers — Free Whites

Slaves — Unfree Blacks

Since the planters and overseers were both members of the free white caste, then qualitative and quantitative similarities may have appeared in the housing, artifacts, and foods at the planter and overseer sites. If so, the archaeological remains at these sites would reflect the racial/legal similarities existing between the free white planters and overseers.

Second, the plantation inhabitants differed in social or occupational status. The planters were managers, the overseers were field supervisors, and most of the slaves were agricultural workers.

Social Status

Planters — Managers

Overseers — Supervisors

Slaves — Workers

If qualitative and quantitative differences appeared in the archaeological remains at the three sites, then the archaeological remains would reflect the social differences existing among the plantation inhabitants.

Third, it was possible that the elite planter family regarded both hired overseers and slaves as subordinates.

Elite/Subordinate Status

Planters — Elite

Owners and Slaves — Subordinates

Overseers were held in low esteem by their planter employers; and overseers had little job security or dignity despite the valuable services they performed on plantations (Scarborough 1964). Most overseers at Cannon's Point lasted only a year or two before they were fired. Furthermore, they received only a few hundred dollars in exchange for their services (Couper 1839-54). Despite their supervisory roles and their middle class farming backgrounds (Scarborough 1966: 5), overseers' material living conditions may have approximated those of the slaves. If qualitative and quantitative similarities appeared in the archaeological remains at the slave and overseer sites, then the archaeological remains would reflect the subordinate status of both slaves and overseers.

The comparison of the antebellum housing, artifacts, and foods at the Cannon's Point Plantation revealed that the archaeological record reflected all three kinds of status differences.

The housing of the plantation inhabitants generally reflected racial/legal status differences. In terms of construction materials and techniques, expected durability, living space, and conveniences, the large, well-built overseers' house more closely resembled the planters' luxurious house than the small one-room slave cabin. The overseers' house may have been a visible symbol of white racial solidarity for the benefit of the dozens of black slaves living on the plantation.

The artifacts at the plantation sites, however, reflected all three kinds of status.[1] As an example, the liquor bottles from the sites reflected racial/legal status. Fragments of case bottles, which commonly held gin, were relatively more common in the white planter (17%) and overseer (10%) antebellum refuse than in the black slave refuse (4%). Also, fragments of dark olive-green bottles, which commonly held ale, porter, cider, and wines, were relatively more common in the slave antebellum refuse (84%) than in the overseer (74%) and planter (73%) refuse. In turn, the ceramic forms from the plantation sites reflected social status. At the planters' kitchen, transfer-printed plates, soup-plates, and platters composed 62 per cent of the identifiable tableware forms. At the overseers' house, transfer-printed serving flatware composed about 28 per cent of the tableware forms. And at the slave cabin, transfer-printed serving flatware composed only 19 per cent of the tableware forms (Otto in South 1977: Table 5.6). Finally, the ceramic types reflected subordinate and elite differences. At the slave and overseer sites, blue transfer-printed pearlware and whiteware composed about 21 per cent and 14 per cent of the total sherds from the antebellum refuse. But at the planter's kitchen, blue transfer-printed pearlware and whiteware composed 77 per cent of the total antebellum sherds (Otto in South 1977: Table 5.1).

The food remains from the plantation sites reflected both racial/legal and elite/subordinate status. The black slaves, for example, were more dependent on wild animals to supplement their diet than either the white overseers or planters. Converting the bone weights of identifiable food animals to their equivalent edible meat weights revealed that wild animals composed 45 per cent of the slave meat diet. In contrast, wild animal meat composed less than 40 per cent of the estimated overseer and planter meat diets. Nevertheless, both slaves and overseers ate the same limited range of wild animals. There were only twenty-four and twenty-two genera and species of wild mammals, fish, and turtles in the slave and overseer refuse. Conversely, there were thirty-five genera and species of wild animals in the planter's refuse. The distribution of wild animal taxa at the plantation sites clearly reflected subordinate and elite status differences.

The planter family could appoint several slaves to hunt and fish to supply the planter's table with game and seafood. The planter's slave hunters and fishermen had time to visit the outlying habitats. They frequently fished in the sounds and the landward marshes, and they hunted on the barrier islands, collecting a wide variety of the available animal species. The slaves and overseers, however, had to collect their own food during their leisure hours. Since they were only part-time food collectors, they hunted and trapped in the forests on Cannon's Point; and they fished in the tidal creeks surrounding the plantation. As a result, they collected a more limited variety of game, fish, turtles.

Not only did the slaves and overseers have limited time for food collecting, but they also had limited time for food preparation and a limited variety of cooking utensils. Given this situation, the slaves and overseers may have combined their grains, meats, and vegetables in "seemingly incongruous mixtures" in iron cooking pots, forming pottages, rice perlous, and stews. These one-pot meals could be left simmering for hours, while the slaves and overseers engaged in other work (Booth 1971: 17; Hilliard 1972: 49, 62). One ex-slave from South Carolina described such a meal: "The whole [stew] had been boiled . . . until the flesh had disappeared from the bones, which were broken in small pieces—a flitch of bacon, some green corn, squashes, tomatoes, and onions had been added. . . . " (Ball 1859: 139).

The zooarchaeological and archaeological evidence from Cannon's Point indicated the slaves and overseers often ate such one pot meals. To obtain more nourishment from their limited meat, the slaves and overseers cleaved open the bones and stewed them with the meat, vegetables, and grains. No saw marks were present on the bones in the slave and overseer antebellum refuse; apparently, the meat was not divided up into regular cuts and joints for roasting. Rather, there were axe and knife marks on the broken large mammal bones, which had been cooked up in stews.

The slaves and overseers served up their liquid-based food, with its "spoon meat," in banded ware serving bowls; and they sopped up the pot liquor with bread made from cornmeal and rice flour, which was baked in the hearths. At the slave and overseer sites, banded ware serving bowls were relatively common, composing 29 per cent and 17 per cent of the ceramic forms (Otto in South 1977: 103-104, Table 5.6).

But at the planter's kitchen, banded ware bowl forms were very rare, composing only 6 per cent of the ceramic forms. Also, relatively few bones had been cleaved open; instead, saw marks were present on the scapulae, ribs, and vertebrae of large mammals, indicating the carcasses had been carefully butchered to produce roasts for the planter's table. In the planter's dining room, the roast meats were served on transfer-printed platters, following the first course of seafood-and meat-based soups served in tureens. The planter family ate these foods from transfer-printed plates and soup-plates rather than serving bowls (Otto in South 1977: 104-105, Table 5.6). Therefore, the food preparation and consumption habits of the plantation inhabitants reflected elite and subordinate status, since the food habits of the planter family differed markedly from those of the slaves and overseers.

The controlled comparison of the food remains, artifacts, and housing from Cannon's Point sites demonstrated that archaeologists cannot always accurately infer the status of former site inhabitants from the quality and quantity of archaeological remains. At Cannon's Point, certain kinds of archaeological evidence reflected certain kinds of status; and some categories of archaeological evidence did not reflect any status patterning. In complex societies such as the Old South, the problem of status patterning at archaeological sites becomes highly complex.

Rather than speculating about the status of site inhabitants, archaeologists should attempt to identify the true status of the site inhabitants by using documents, oral testimony, or other means. Then, by holding status as a known constant, it should be possible to explain differences and similarities in the archaeological record by referring to known status. With documentary controls, we can demonstrate how differences in known status produce patterning in the archaeological record. To quote Garry Wheeler Stone: "The occupation, wealth, social status, and ethnic background of a household is of the same class of information as the statistical distribution of their archaeologically recovered trash." (Stone 1970: 126)

Acknowledgments

I wish to thank Charles Fairbanks, Professor of Anthropology, University of Florida, for reading and commenting on earlier versions of this paper. Charles Fairbanks pioneered plantation archaeology with his excavations at Kingsley Plantation, Ft. George Island, Florida, and Rayfield Plantation, Cumberland Island, Georgia. His articles on slave cabin archaeology (Fairbanks 1974; Ascher and Fairbanks 1971) were the source of many of the research hypotheses for the Cannon's Point excavations.

Notes

[1] The differences in the frequencies of artifact types were tested with the chi-square statistic to determine significance.

Bibliography

Ascher, Robert and Charles H. Fairbanks
   1971   Excavation of a Slave Cabin: Georgia, USA. *Historical Archaeology* 5: 3-17.

Ball, Charles
   1859   *Fifty Years in Chains; or the Life of an American Slave.* Dayton, New York.

Bonner, James C.
   1965   Plantation and Farm: The Agricultural South. In *Writing Southern History Essays in Honor of Fletcher M. Green* edited by Arthur S. Link and Rembert W. Patrick. Louisiana State University Press, Baton Rouge.

Booth, Sally S.
   1971   *Hung, Strung, and Potted: A History of Eating in Colonial America.* Clarkson N. Potter, New York.

Couper, James H.
   1826-52   Hopeton [and Cannon's Point] Plantation Account Book. James H. Couper Plantation Records # 185, Southern Historical Collection, University of North Carolina at Chapel Hill.
   1839-54   Hopeton [Cannon's Point] Plantation Journal. Ibid.

Craven, Avery O.
   1930   Poor Whites and Negroes in the Antebellum South. *Journal of Negro History* 15: 14-25.

Fairbanks, Charles H.
   MS   The Strategy of Digging in St. Augustine. Paper Presented at the Annual Meeting of the Society for Historical Archaeology, Tallahassee, Florida, 1972.
   1974   The Kingsley Slave Cabins in Duval County, Florida, 1968. *The Conference on Historic Site Archaeology Papers 1972* 7: 62-93.
   1976   Spaniards, Planters, Ships, and Slaves: Historical Archaeology in Florida and Georgia. *Archaeology* 29: 165-172.

Genovese, Eugene D.
   1974   *Roll, Jordan, Roll.* Pantheon Books, New York.

Hilliard, Sam B.
   1972   *Hogmeat and Hoecake: Food Supply in the Old South 1840-1860* Southern Illinois University Press, Carbondale.

Laumann, Edward O. and others (eds.)
   1970   *The Logic of Social Hierarchies.* Markham Publishing Co., Chicago.

Otto, John S.
   1977   Artifacts and Status Differences—A Comparison of Ceramics from Planter, Overseer, and Slave Sites on an Antebellum Plantation. In *Research Strategies in Historical Archaeology* edited by Stanley South. Academic Press, New York.

Scarborough, William K.
   1974   The Plantation Overseer: A Re-evaluation. *Agricultural History* 38: 13-20.

Scarborough, William K.
   1966   *The Overseer: Plantation Management in the Old South.* Louisiana State University Press, Baton Rouge.

South, Stanley A.
   1972   Evolution and Horizon as Revealed in Ceramic Analysis in Historical Archaeology. *The Conference on Historic Site Archaeology Papers 1971* 6: 71-106.

Stone, Garry W.
   1970   Reply to Cleland. *The Conference on Historic Site Archaeology Papers 1968* 3: 124-126.

Trigger, Bruce G.
   1968   The Determinants of Settlement Pattern. In *Settlement Archaeology* edited by K. C. Chang. National Press Books, Palo Alto, California.

Tumin, Melvin M.
   1967   *Social Stratification: The Forms and Functions of Inequality.* Prentice-Hall, Inc., Englewood Cliffs, New Jersey.

US Coast Survey
   1869   Map of Altamaha Sound and Vicinity. On file at the Margaret Davis Cate Collection, Brunswick Junior College, Brunswick, Georgia.

Wall, Bennett H.
   1965   African Slavery. In *Writing Southern History.*

Warner, W. Lloyd
   1970   The Study of Social Stratification. In *Readings on Social Stratification* edited by Melvin Tumin. Prentice-Hall Inc. Englewood Cliffs, New Jersey.

Wolf, Eric R.
   1959   Aspects of Plantation Systems in the New World: Community Sub-Cultures and Social Classes. In *Seminar on Plantation Systems of the New World.* Social Science Monographs 7. Research Institute for the Study of Man and the Pan American Union, Washington, D.C.

CHAPTER 2
Looking for the "Afro" in Colono-Indian Pottery
LELAND FERGUSON

Colono-Indian pottery was formally described by Ivor Noel-Hume in 1962. Noel-Hume was familiar with unglazed, low-fired, plain earthenwares that he had found at Williamsburg and that had been found at many other colonial sites from the Carolinas to Delaware. The most common vessel form was described as a simple, flat-bottomed bowl, but he mentioned that sometimes forms that were imitations of European vessels appeared. Because the material was somewhat similar to both prehistoric and historic (19th century) Indian wares in Virginia, he called the pottery Colono-Indian ware. He used this name despite his belief that the ware continued to be made after the colonial period.

Although Noel-Hume thought the ware to have been made by Indians, he considered it to have been used by Afro-American slaves. A synopsis of his reasoning (Noel-Hume 1962: 5) follows:

1. The unglazed ware is inferior to glazed wares.
2. Glazed wares were within the financial reach of all except the poorest colonists.
3. That the unglazed ware is found in towns and wealthy plantation sites implies that both have a common point to which the ware was applicable.
4. Slaves would have developed European tastes in ways of cooking and table wares.
5. Slave holders would not likely have purchased glazed vessels for use by slaves.

His conclusion was that the slaves used ceramic vessels made by Indians. He wrote (Noel-Hume 1962: 5) that, "the astute Indians may have found a useful market amongst the slaves and would have tailored their wares to styles acceptable to these customers."

Noel-Hume's contention that the pottery was made by Indians was based on ethnographic descriptions of Pamunkey pottery manufacture in Virginia (Speck 1928, Stern 1951). References to similar pottery may also be found for the Catawba (Fewkes 1944, Harrington 1908) as well as for other Indian tribes stretching to the lower Mississippi River Valley (Swanton 1946: 549).

Since Noel-Hume's original description, two short studies of Colono-Indian ware in the Atlantic coastal area have been published (Binford 1965, Baker 1972). In the first of these, Binford (1965) describes imitation European vessels from an Indian site in eastern Virginia. In the other, Baker (1972) treats the historic trade of pottery by the Catawba Indians of South Carolina. Beyond these two major works, several shorter references concerning Colono-Indian wares from many parts of the Southeast have appeared (e.g. Florida: Fairbanks 1962; Tennessee: Polhemus 1977; South Carolina: South 1974, Lees and Kimery-Lees n.d.).

Polhemus (1977) and South (1974) have suggested that the wares may have been made by Afro-Americans. This suggestion was based upon a casual observation of the similarity of modern Ghanaian and Nigerian pottery to the Colono-Indian ware of South Carolina. With this important observation the lid was cracked on a box of ideas that has sat covered with dust in the darkest corner of North American historic sites archaeology—the contribution of Afro-Americans to the pottery we call "Colono-Indian."

Reconsidering the Colono-Indian Ware

Beginning the reconsideration of Colono-Indian ware, there are two major questions that need to be answered. They are:

1. Who made the pottery we call Colono-Indian ware and when did they make it?
2. Who used the pottery and what were their patterns of selection?

Who made it and when?

It is possible that all three of the major ethnic groups in eastern North America made the wares, but I think we can rule out Euro-Americans since they dominated the ceramic market with European products. The wares were most certainly made by either Indians or Afro-Americans.

There is clear and well-documented evidence that Indians have made pottery that fits the general category "Colono-Indian." Catawba vessels are presently on sale in gift shops and museums throughout the eastern United States.

Furthermore, there is documentation of the manufacture and sale of these items by Catawba Indians stretching back to the early 19th century (Harrington 1908, Speck 1928, Fewkes 1944, Stern 1951, Baker 1972), and there is at least one reference to late 18th century manufacture and sale (Simms 1841).

In the far western portion of the eastern United States, ware made by Indians in imitation of European forms was described in the 18th century when Du Pratz (1758: 178-179) (see also Swanton 1911, p. 2 and Swanton 1946, p. 549) stated that the Natchez, "also [made] dishes and plates like those of the French." Du Pratz goes on to say that as a curiosity he had the Indians make him some pottery modeled on his own European earthenware. Neitzel (1965: 45-47, 54, 87) has recovered vessels with shapes similar to European forms from the Fatherland Site—the Grand Village of the Natchez in the present state of Mississippi. Types from Georgia, Florida or Alabama including Kasita Red Filmed (Jennings and Fairbanks 1940), Mission Red Filmed (Smith 1948), and San Marcos Plain and Red (Goggin 1952) show some formal similarities to European ceramics. However, these types are associated with other traits such as incising and paddle stamping that are obviously within the American Indian ceramic tradition. These materials are not usually included within the Colono-Indian rubric established by Noel-Hume.

Although detailed information for comparison has yet to be extracted and presented, there is an obvious qualitative difference between the Indian wares from the Gulf coastal areas and the Colono-Indian materials of the middle Atlantic coast. Paradoxically, in the middle Atlantic coastal area there are few traditional American Indian traits associated with Colono-Indian pottery, and the only archaeological association from the colonial period of Colono-Indian wares with Indians has come from the site of the Nottoway and Weanoc Indians of southeastern Virginia (Binford 1965). Importantly, there was Indian-African admixture among the people responsible for creating this archaeological site (Lewis Binford, personal communication, 1978).

Thus, both the historical and archaeological evidence show that during the early colonial period some American Indian groups of the Gulf coastal plain were making pottery that seems related to European wares. In the middle Atlantic coastal area there is clear historical evidence of Indians making Colono-Indian wares in the late 18th, 19th, and 20th centuries. On the other hand, the tie of Indians to the production of these wares in the first half of the 18th century on the middle Atlantic coastal plain is weak; and the style of Colono-Indian ware, once it is firmly associated with Indians of the Carolinas and Virginia, bears only slight resemblance to prehistoric Indian materials. Furthermore, the materials are not commonly similar to any specific European forms.

In excavations at the original site of Charles Towne in South Carolina, Stanley South (1971: 102-105, and personal communication, 1978) found Colono-Indian ware in the fortification ditch that the colonists cut across Albemarle Point. This ditch was constructed in 1670 and began to fill in by

1680. From archaeological evidence, South believes the ditch to have filled within a few years. Thus, in the first decade of the South Carolina colony, fully developed Colono-Indian ware appeared within the town.

In subsequent work at the Indian site adjacent to the site of the original Charles Towne, South (personal communication, 1978) reports several pits containing colonial period Indian ceramics of the York Ware Group (South 1976: 28-29). One of these pits contained a small sliver of glass among the Indian sherds, and a charcoal sample from the pit has give a date of A.D. 1770 ±80. All of these ceramics were prehistoric in style. There was no Colono-Indian pottery in this collection of late Indian material from a site adjacent to the early site of Charles Towne.

To date there is no known Indian site of the colonial period in South Carolina that has produced Colono-Indian pottery. The Scott's Lake Site (Ferguson 1973, 1975) is probably a site visited by John Lawson in 1701 when he made his famous trip through the Carolinas (Baker 1974). Examination of thousands of sherds from this site has so far failed to reveal any sherds of Colono-Indian ware. Likewise, David Phelps of East Carolina University in North Carolina (personal communication, 1978) reports no indication of Colono-Indian ware being associated with known Indian sites in his recent researches. It seems that in the Carolinas and Virginia, the Nottoway and Weanoc materials excavated by Binford (1965) are the only examples of Colono-Indian wares being found in known Indian sites of the 17th or 18th centuries, and there were Afro-Americans living at this site.

While Colono-Indian artifacts have little representation on Indian sites, they are consistently found on Euro-American and Afro-American sites of the 17th, 18th and 19th centuries (see Baker 1972 and Noel-Hume 1962). Thus, the archaeological record seems to be telling us that while history reports that these wares are associated with Indians during the last two hundred years, they are firmly associated with Euro-Americans and Afro-Americans during the first century of occupation. In other words, during the early part of the occupation of the Carolinas and Virginia, the archaeological record indicates that these wares are more closely associated with non-Indians than with Indians. Since Euro-Americans had their own ceramic traditions which arrived in this continent fully intact, the archaeological implication is that these wares were made by Afro-Americans.

Afro-Americans came to this continent with a long tradition of producing low-fired earthenwares (e.g. Mathewson 1974, Mathewson and Flight 1972). In West Africa where the majority of North American slaves originated (Bean 1975, Herskovits 1964: 116-117), there are well-developed techniques of pottery manufacture, and some villages specialize in the manufacture of these wares. Archaeological evidence indicates that trade in special ceramics extends at least to the 15th and 16th centuries (Mathewson and Flight 1972), and it is probably older than this. Of contemporary groups, Forde (1970) mentions that among the Nupe of the Niger-Benue confluence, the villages of Jebba Island, Baro, Badeggi and Bida are famous for their pottery and they have a regular trade in both pots and clay. The main products are reported to be small water jugs and large water containers. Talbot (1968: 115) states that, "From the Congo to the Niger and the Nile the pottery of Mangbutu [in southern Nigeria] is superior to that of any other."

These contemporary references together with the archaeological references give testimony to the firm tradition of manufacturing low-fired earthenware in West Africa. Certainly many of the Africans, brought to this country as slaves, brought knowledge of the well-developed technology of West African pottery production with them.

As I have mentioned earlier, Polhemus (1977) has noted the similarity between Colono-Indian vessels and artifacts from Ghana. He states (Polhemus 1977: 314):

> The Ghana vessels are flat bottomed, fine grit or sand tempered, plain burnished, and bear the incised 'X' on the base which many 'Colono-Indian' vessels from South Carolina also possess. Other than through a detailed analysis of the composition of paste and temper the Ghana sample could not be differentiated from vessels excavated in South Carolina.

One alternative hypothesis may be that the modern African vessels and the Colono-Indian vessels are similar because in each region the manufacturers tried to imitate European forms. The result would be a similarity due to a common stimulus rather than direct connection. For clarification we need to look at the prehistoric repertoire of African potters in comparison to Colono-Indian materials to see how much the former may have influenced the latter.

Of the Colono-Indian ware from Virginia, Noel-Hume (1962: 7) states:

> It is certainly true that some of the more elaborate shapes can be identified with European prototypes, but the vast majority of the vessels have only two features in common with any European ware, a flat bottom and a slightly everted rim that is more sophisticated than those that occurred on prehistoric forms. [Here Noel-Hume is referring to prehistoric forms of Indian vessels from eastern Virginia].

He continues:

> These features, particularly, the flattening of the base, mark a turning point in the evolution of Virginia Indian pottery and it is reasonable to suppose that that change would not have occurred when it did, were it not for the advent of European colonists. This, in my view, is as far as one can safely go in endowing the simple bowl shapes with European characteristics.

From South Carolina, flat bottoms and bowl forms also seem to be common Colono-Indian characteristics (Baker 1972). From the Cambridge cellar, a site occupied in the latter part of the 18th century, Baker (1972: 24-25) identified eleven of the thirteen identifiable forms as bowls, and seven of these bowls were identified as being flat-bottomed.

Flat-bottomed bowls are present in southeastern North America in prehistoric times (see Caldwell 1958 for some examples), but they are never a common prehistoric trait along the Atlantic coastal plain. Additionally, an examination of West African archaeological reports reveals that there are examples of flat-bottomed bowls from that area that date as early as the time of Christ. Mathewson (1974: 155) illustrates bowls from northern Ghana that have flat bases and flaring rims. Profiles of these African vessels are quite similar to profiles shown by both Baker (1972: 23) and Noel-Hume (1962: 10). These comparisons indicate that the basic form of what appears to be the majority of 18th century Colono-Indian ware was known in prehistoric times in Africa as well as parts of southeastern North America. The flat bottomed bowls showing up in South Carolina and Virginia may have nothing to do with European imitations, and they could relate to a continuation of the lengthy African ceramic tradition.

The decorative techniques of both Colono-Indian pottery and historic Indian pottery may well point to the influence of African pottery. In West Africa the most common techniques for decoration and surface finishing are burnishing, incising, and impressing designs with a roulette (Cardew 1970: 12-13). The burnishing is done with a small pebble or with a string of baobab seeds. Rouletting is done with a small carved stick or a small length of plaited fiber (Leith-Ross 1970: 185; Dark 1973: 71-73). The designs of carved roulettes include bold checks, diamonds and complex patterns of vertical, horizontal and diagonal lines.

Rouletting was so popular in West Africa that when maize, a New World plant, was introduced, it created a stir in the pottery industry. Corn cobs served as ready made roulettes, and archaeologists in Africa use cob marked or impressed pottery as a horizon marker (Willet 1962, Stanton 1963) for the colonial period. In North America it has been noted that even though maize is an ancient plant, cob impressed pottery is rather recent. In the type description of Dan River ceramics from North Carolina, Coe and Lewis (1952) commented:

> The use of corncobs to roughen the exterior surfaces of pottery vessels was general practice among historic tribes in the Southeast, although it never appeared to produce a dominant type of surface finish. Alachua Cob Marked in Florida occupies a comparable position [to Dan River Cob Impressed from North Carolina]. Cob marking has been frequently observed in Georgia and southern Virginia but usually incorrectly labeled net impressed, finger nail punctations or walnut roughened. In all cases it appears in the historic context.

Examination of the "Southeastern Bibliography of Pottery Type Descriptions" reveals eight east coast types that have cob surface finishing (Broyles 1967): Alachua, Clarks Hill, Dan River, Caraway, Clarksville, Pensacola, St. Johns, and Etowah. With two exceptions, St. Johns and Etowah, all of these have been demonstrated to be from the historic period. Thus, in a collection of pottery type descriptions that extends north to Virginia and Kentucky and west to Texas, corn cob surface finish on pottery has been identified in Virginia, North Carolina, South Carolina, Georgia, and Florida. These states were colonized early and were the focus of slave importation into the Southeast.

Not only does there seem to be a flourish of cob marking in the Southeast during the colonial period, but there is also a revival of check stamping during the historic period (Caldwell 1950: 7-8). In some cases this new check stamping is large and bold and reminiscent of the check stamping seen on modern African vessels and applied with a roulette (Leith-Ross 1970: 185; Dark 1973: Plates 178-181).

The study of Colono-Indian pottery at this stage is full of paradoxes, and this consideration of surface treatment is another example. There is little doubt that the pottery we call Colono-Indian was made by either Afro-Americans or American Indians. Both of these groups have a tradition of manufacturing plain and burnished ceramics, so the finish of the ware could have come from either tradition. On the other hand, both traditions also expressed a rich variety of other surface finishes that are not commonly found on Colono-Indian ware. When other finishing traits similar to those in West Africa such as check stamping and cob marking are seen in the Southeast, they occur not on Colono-Indian ware but on ceramics that come from sites attributed to American Indians. Perhaps when we begin to understand this paradox we shall begin to understand more fully the nature of the relationship between the three ethnic groups in the southeastern portion of North America during the colonial period.

Combining this evidence for the Afro-American manufacture of some Colono-Indian ware, we see most importantly that African people had a long tradition of manufacturing low-fired coiled and molded earthenwares and that the archaeological materials from the early colonial period are consistently found on sites occupied by Afro-Americans. The predominant vessel forms are similar to those made in Africa in prehistoric times and the major method of surface finishing which is plain (smoothed) or burnished is common in prehistoric Africa. Not only is the early Colono-Indian ware reminiscent of African wares, but African ceramic styles may have influenced American Indian wares in the case of cob marking and the revival of check stamping.

Who used the ware?

The problem of who used the Colono-Indian ware is not quite so confusing as the question of who made it. The people who used the ware dropped pieces of broken ceramics around their occupation sites, and these broken pieces are easily retrieved through archaeological research. We have only to identify the occupants to identify the users of the pottery. Beyond this excellent archaeological record, we have some historical references to the people who used Colono-Indian ware as well as some first-hand experience.

Today, users of Catawba pottery, which is made in the Colono-Indian pottery tradition, are members of the general public who buy pieces as curios. For the late 18th and early 19th century, Baker (1972: 13-15) has compiled information indicating that the Catawba Indians sold their wares to both White and Black people in trading trips to the coastal plain. Baker infers from the frequency of references that more Black people bought the wares than Whites. Although there is no quantitative data to support this interpretation, I feel Baker is correct. Likewise, we do not have an quantitative data to determine the proportion of Colono-Indian ceramics used by either Black or White people. I suppose that the poorest people of both groups were using the majority of Colono-Indian ware, although some more "well-to-do" people may have used it for specialty cooking. William Gilmore Simms (1841: 122) stated that, "it was a confident faith among the old ladies, that okra soup was always inferior if cooked in any but an Indian pot." (Interestingly, okra is an African plant.)

In examination of South Carolina and North Carolina archaeological reports, I find that there is a paucity of Colono-Indian ware from domestic and military sites of the 19th century. South and Widmer's (1977) careful subsurface survey of Fort Johnson in South Carolina revealed no Colono-Indian pottery at that Civil War site. The excavation of three early to mid-19th century sites in the piedmont has likewise produced no Colono-Indian pottery. Excavations at Pinckneyville in Union County (Carrillo 1972), the Howser House in Cherokee County (Carrillo 1976), and a house in Brattonsville in York County (Wilkins, Hunter and Carrillo 1976) failed to recover a single sherd of Colono-Indian pottery even though these sites were located only a few miles from the heartland of the Catawba Nation. Farther to the west in Spartanburg County, Stanley South found no Colono-Indian pottery at the Price House (South 1970). Lees and Kimery-Lees' recent study (n.d.) of Limerick Plantation near Charleston, South Carolina has revealed a definite drop in the frequency of Colono-Indian ceramics in the 19th century on that plantation. The only possible 19th century occurrences of Colono-Indian pottery are from the Cambridge Cellar (Baker 1972) in Greenwood County and the Kershaw House in Camden (Lewis 1977). If the Colono-Indian materials from these sites do date to the 19th century, they are early, and it is more likely that the artifacts from both sites are from the 18th century.

Thus, while there are references to the 19th century use of Colono-Indian pottery, the archaeological material is infrequent and suggests that there is a greater frequency of material from the early part of the century. The combined historical and archaeological data suggest that even though the piedmont

Catawba Indians were making some Colono-Indian pottery during the 19th century, the majority of the wares were being used in the coastal plain—most probably by poor people, most probably slaves.

Without a doubt the 18th century is the "century of Colono-Indian pottery." While there is a dearth of Colono-Indian pottery from 19th century sites, scarcely a non-Indian 18th century site has been excavated in South Carolina and coastal North Carolina that has not produced sherds of this ware (see also Binford 1965: 86). Of sixteen late 17th and 18th century sites in South Carolina for which I could find data, fourteen produced Colono-Indian ware. In many cases it was in great profusion.

In the excavation of Fort Moultrie of the Revolutionary War, South (1974: 181) reports that 37 per cent of all ceramics recovered were Colono-Indian ware. (Contrast this to the absence of Colono-Indian ware from Fort Johnson of the Civil War.)

On other sites of the 18th century, Colono-Indian ware shows up in varying frequencies with the high being that represented at Fort Moultrie. The remainder of the ceramics from these 18th century sites are imported wares from Europe. My feeling at this point is that the occurrence of Colono-Indian ware on these sites represents a scarcity of ceramics; the pattern of occurrence suggesting that they were more scarce during the 18th century, the colonial period, than during the 19th century. This scarcity was probably most strongly felt by poor people who resorted to their own resources as well as those of their neighbors to meet their needs; the Colono-Indian pottery of the 18th century seems to reflect that resort.

The Black Potters of the West Indies

South's recovery of well-developed Colono-Indian ware from the fortification ditch at the early settlement of Charles Towne helps draw our attention toward the possible non-Indian origin of these wares. Interestingly, many of Charles Towne's early settlers came not from England but from the established colony of Barbados (Wood 1974), and while we do not have any direct historical reference to slaves making pottery in South Carolina, there is evidence of their early association with this craft in Barbados (Handler and Lange 1978: 135-144).

Two types of pottery manufacture, wheel-made and coiled or molded pottery, were engaged in by the slaves of the Lesser Antilles including Barbados. The manufacture of wheel-made sugar pots is recorded as early as the period between 1650 and 1670. Historical references mention slaves using their own wares by the fourth and fifth decades of the 18th century. (Certainly this activity may be much earlier than the first historical reference.) Beyond this, there is evidence of slave potters and more recent non-slave potters manufacturing pottery using non-kiln and non-wheel technology on the islands of Antigua and Nevis (Handler and Lange 1978: 140-141; Handler 1964).

Wood points out that many of the early settlers from Barbados settled in South Carolina. The historical references mentioned by Handler and Lange clearly suggest that the slaves who accompanied these settlers may well have been engaging in the manufacture of pottery in a slave context prior to their arrival in the Carolina colony. Thus, while we have no direct historical reference to these people's making pottery in South Carolina there is evidence from the colonies in the Lesser Antilles.

The Importance of Style in Colono-Indian Pottery

In conclusion I would like to comment on the importance of the evolution and diversity of style in Colono-Indian pottery. Within this easily formed artifact are the expressions of thousands of common people. Both Afro-Americans and American Indians may have had a hand in creating the wares. European artifacts provided some models for imitation, and whoever selected the vessels for use—whether they were Red, Black, or White—helped direct the course of this evolution.

The production of these wares involved a plastic medium and they were easily made. As personal tastes or markets changed, potters could have easily altered the production of their wares. Crafters could have imitated European forms, Indian forms or African forms, or they could have made up new styles in the course of production. It would be quite interesting to see the difference between the forms used by Whites, Blacks, and Indians at the same point in time. The difference in form should represent the difference in concepts of style and function among the different groups.

For this type of study, determination of the temporal placement of these wares is not difficult. We are able to date 18th and 19th century sites with great accuracy. Ceramics including Colono-Indian ware are frequently found and they are well preserved. In many cases, the beginning of such a study will involve simply looking at previously published reports. Expansion of the study will involve the investigation of many archaeological sites in the Southeastern United States.

"Well, What Are We Going to Call It Now?"

My primary purpose in presenting this information has been to encourage archaeologists to use more imagination when considering the ware we have been calling Colono-Indian. The suffix, Indian, while not incorrect in all cases, unduly limits this pottery. Although I am not excited about contributing a new name to add to the mass of coined verbiage in the archaeological literature, many archaeologists have asked me, "Well, what are we going to call it now?"

I think Noel-Hume was correct when he used the prefix "Colono" for the wares he found in Virginia. Even though he knew then and we know now that these types of wares were made after the Revolution, the birth and primary use of this ware in the New World was certainly during the colonial period. The problem seems to be only with the suffix. Polhemus (1977) has suggested by use (although not too seriously) that this ware be called "Colono-Black." However, since we know some wares of this style to have been made by Indians, this name also seems inappropriate.

Perhaps the best course is to drop the suffix and simply call the ware "Colono Ware." Certainly the correct usage would be Colonial Ware, but that sounds rather stuffy and also as if it were ware produced in the Mother Country for use in the colonies or ware produced by the colonies as an important export. On the other hand, "Colono Ware" has a casual sound befitting a product that was casually produced to fit the everyday needs of the populace. Besides, it has the advantage of dropping a word from the archaeological lexicon.

Summary

In summary, the most frequent occurrence of Colono Ware in the Southeast is in the late 17th and 18th centuries. Lesser amounts appear in archaeological sites of the 19th century and some of the wares continue to be made today. The frequency of occurrence of the pottery is probably directly related to shortages of glazed wares.

We are sure that some Indians made this pottery throughout the historic period. However, this material is most frequently found on Afro-American and Euro-American sites of the 17th and 18th centuries. West Africans have a long tradition of producing early forms of Colono Ware, and I believe it a reasonable hypothesis that Afro-American slaves made much if not most of the Colono Ware we see in the archaeological record.

There are historical references to all three major ethnic groups in the Southeast being involved with either the production or use of Colono Ware. Thus, the form of the wares found on archaeological sites of these ethnic groups should represent their tastes in style and concerns for function. Studies of dated collections of Colono materials should help significantly in evaluating the changing conceptual worlds of the three diverse groups of people brought together in southeastern North America.

Bibliography

Baker, Steven G.
- 1972 Colono-Indian pottery from Cambridge, South Carolina with comments on the historic Catawba pottery trade. Institute of Archeology and Anthropology, *Notebook*, Vol. IV, No. 1, p. 3. University of South Carolina.
- 1974 Cofitachique: fair province of Carolina. Unpublished Master's Thesis. Department of History, University of South Carolina.

Bean Richard Nelson
- 1975 *The British Trans-Atlantic Slave Trade, 1650-1775*. Arno Press, New York.

Binford, Lewis R.
- 1965 Colonial period ceramics of the Nottoway and Weanoc Indians of southeastern Virginia. *Quarterly Bulletin, Archaeological Society of Virginia*, Vol. 19, No. 4.

Braunholtz, H. J.
- 1934 Wooden roulettes for impressing patterns on pottery. *Man*, No. 107, p. 81.

Broyles, Bettye, Editor
- 1967 Bibliography of pottery type descriptions. *Southeastern Archaeological Conference, Bulletin*, No. 4.

Caldwell, Joseph R.
- 1950 A preliminary report on excavations in the Allatoona reservoir. *Early Georgia*, Vol. I, No. 1, pp. 5-22. University of Georgia, Athens, Georgia.
- 1958 Trend and tradition in the prehistory of the eastern United States. *American Anthropologist*, Vol. 60, No. 6, Pt. 2, *American Anthropological Association Memoir*, No. 88; and *Illinois State Museum Scientific Papers*, Vol. 10. Menasha.

Cardew, Michael
- 1970 Introduction: pottery techniques in Nigeria. In *Nigerian Pottery*, by Sylvia Leith-Ross. Ibadan University Press, Ibadan, Nigeria, pp. 9-13.

Carrillo, Richard
- 1972 Archeological excavation at Pinckneyville, site of Pinckney District, 1791-1800. Research Manuscript Series, No. 25, Institute of Archeology and Anthropology, University of South Carolina, Columbia.
- 1976 The Howser house and the chronicle grave and mass burial, King's Mountain National Military Park, South Carolina. Research Manuscript Series, No. 102, Institute of Archeology and Anthropology, University of South Carolina, Columbia.

Coe, Joffre L. and Ernest Lewis
- 1952 Dan River series statement. In *Historic Pottery of the Eastern U.S.*, edited by James B. Griffin. Museum of Anthropology, University of Michigan, Ann Arbor.

Dark, Philip J. C.
    1973   *An Introduction to Benin Art and Technology.* Oxford/Clarendon Press.
Dumont de Montigny
    1753   *Memoires Historiques sur la Louisiane.* Edited by Le Maserier. 2 Vols. Paris.
Fairbanks, Charles
    1962   A Colono-Indian ware milk pitcher. *The Florida Anthropologist,* Vol. XV, No. 4. Gainesville.
Ferguson, Leland
    1973   Exploratory archeology at the Scott's Lake site, Santee Indian Mound –Ft. Watson: summer 1972. Research Manuscript Series, No. 36, Institute of Archeology and Anthropology, University of South Carolina, Columbia.
    1975   Archeology at Scott's Lake, exploratory research 1972, 1973. Research Manuscript Series, No. 68. Institute of Archeology and Anthropology, University of South Carolina, Columbia.
Fewkes, Vladmir
    1944   Catawba pottery making. *Proceedings of the American Philosophical Society,* Vol. 88. Philadelphia.
Goggin, John M.
    1952   Space and time perspective in northern St. Johns archaeology, Florida. *Yale University Publications in Anthropology,* No. 47. New Haven, Connecticut.
Forde, Daryll (Editor)
    1970   Peoples of the Niger-Benue confluence. *Ethnographic Survey of Africa,* International African Institute.
Harrington, M. R.
    1908   Catawba potters and their work. *American Anthropologist,* N. S. Vol. 10, No. 3, pp. 399-407.
Herskovits, Melville J.
    1964   *The American Negro.* Indiana University Press, Bloomington.
Heyward, Duncan
    1937   *Seed from Madagascar.* University of North Carolina Press, Chapel Hill.
Holmes, William H.
    1903   Aboriginal pottery of the eastern United States. *20th Annual Report of the Bureau of American Ethnology, 1898-1899.* pp. 1-237.
Jennings, Jesse D. and Charles H. Fairbanks
    1940   Pottery type descriptions. *Southeastern Archeological Conference, Newsletter.* Vol. 2, No. 2.
Kelso, William M.
    1968   *Excavations at the Fort King George Historical Site: Darien, Georgia: the 1967 Survey.* Athens, Georgia.
Lees, William B. and Kathryn M. Kimery-Lees
    In Press   The function of Colono-Indian ceramics: insights from Limerick Plantation. *Historical Archaeology,* Vol. 12.

Leith-Ross, Sylvia
    1970   *Nigerian pottery*. Ibadan University Press, Ibadan, Nigeria.
Le Page Du Pratz, Antoine S.
    1758   *Histoire de la Louisiane*. Paris.
Lewis, Kenneth E.
    1977   A functional study of the Kershaw house site in Camden, South Carolina. Research Manuscript Series, No. 110, Institute of Archeology and Anthropology, University of South Carolina, Columbia.
Mathewson, R. Duncan
    1974   Pottery from the Chuluwasi and Jimasangi river sites, Northern Ghana. *West African Journal of Archeology*, Vol. 4, pp. 149-160.
Mathewson, R. Duncan and Colin Flight
    1972   Kisoto bowls: a fifteenth—and sixteenth—century pottery type in northern Ghana. *West African Journal of Archeology*. Vol. 2, pp. 81-92.
Neitzel, Robert S.
    1965   Archeology of the Fatherland site: the Grand Village of the Natchez. *Anthropological Papers of the American Museum of Natural History*. Vol. 51, part 1. New York.
Noel-Hume, Ivor
    1962   An Indian ware of the Colonial period. *Quarterly Bulletin, Archaeological Society of Virginia*. Vol. 17, No. 1, September.
O'Brien, T. P. and S. Hastings
    1933   Pottery making among the Bakonjo (Uganda). *Man*, No. 202, p. 189.
Otto, John Solomon and Russell Lamar Lewis, Jr.
    1974   A formal and functional analysis of San Marcos pottery from site SA 16-23 St. Augustine, Florida. *Bureau of Historic Sites and Properties, Bulletin*, No. 4. Tallahassee.
Polhemus, Richard R.
    1977   Archaeological investigation of the Tellico Blockhouse site (40MR50): a federal military and trade complex. Report submitted to the Tennessee Valley Authority.
Simms, William Gilmore
    1841   *The Magnolia*. Vol. 3, pp. 222-223.
South, Stanley
    1969   Exploratory archeology at the site of 1670-1680 Charles Towne on Albemarle point in South Carolina. Research Manuscript Series, No. 1, Institute of Archeology and Anthropology, University of South Carolina, Columbia.
    1971   Exploratory excavation at the Price House. Research Manuscript Series, No. 5, Institute of Archeology and Anthropology, University of South Carolina, Columbia.
    1971   Archeology at the Charles Towne site (38CH1) on Albemarle point in South Carolina. Part I—the text. Paper of the Institute of Archeology and Anthropology, University of South Carolina, Columbia.
    1974   Palmetto parapets: exploratory archeology at Fort Moultrie, South Carolina, 38CH50. *Occasional Papers of the Institute of Archeology*

and Anthropology, Anthropological Studies No. 1. University of South Carolina, Columbia.

South, Stanley and Randolph Widmer
- 1977 A subsurface sampling strategy for archeological reconnaissance. In *Research Strategies in Historical Archeology,* edited by Stanley South. Academic Press, New York.

Speck, Frank G.
- 1928 Indian notes and monographs. *Museum of the American Indian.* Vol. 1, No. 5.

Stanton,
- 1963 Archeological evidence for changes in maize type in West Africa: an experiment in technique. *Man,* No. 150.

Stern, Theodore
- 1951 Pamunkey pottery making. *Southern Indian Studies,* Vol. 3. Chapel Hill, North Carolina.

Swanton, John R.
- 1911 Indian tribes of the lower Mississippi valley and adjacent coast of the Gulf of Mexico. *Bureau of American Ethnology Bulletin, No. 43.* Washington.
- 1946 *The Indians of the Southeastern United States. Bureau of American Ethnology Bulletin, No. 137.* Washington.

Talbot, Amaury
- 1968 *Woman's Mysteries of a Primitive People: the Ibibios of Southern Nigeria.* Frank Cass and Co. Ltd.

Thomas, N. W.
- 1910 *Pottery-making of the Edo-speaking peoples, southern Nigeria. Man,* Vol. 10, pp. 97-98.

Watkins, C. Malcolm and Ivor Noel-Hume
- 1967 The "poor" potter of Yorktown. *United States National Museum Bulletin 249, Contributions from the Museum of History and Technology, Paper 54,* pp. 73-112.

Wilkins, Joseph C., Howell C. Hunter, and Richard F. Carrillo
- 1975 Historical, architectural and archeological research at Brattonsville, York county, South Carolina. Research Manuscript Series, No. 76, Institute of Archeology and Anthropology, University of South Carolina, Columbia.

Willet, Frank
- 1962 The introduction of maize into West Africa: an assessment of recent evidence. *Africa.* Vol. 32, pp. 1-13.

Wood, Peter H.
- 1974 *Black Majority.* Alfred A. Knopf. New York.

CHAPTER 3

Archaeological Visibility of Afro-American Culture: An Example from Black Lucy's Garden, Andover, Massachusetts[1]

VERNON G. BAKER

Introduction

The persistence of African cultural traits among Black Americans has long been recognized. Elements of present-day Afro-American speech, music, dance, and diet have been identified as African in origin (e.g., Blassingame 1972; Garrett 1966; Lomax 1970). It is likely that during the 18th and 19th centuries such elements were more pronounced than today. As Blassingame writes: "The most remarkable aspect of the whole process of enslavement is the extent to which the American-born slaves were able to retain their ancestors' culture" (1972: 39).

In this paper I discuss the tangible, material ways in which Afro-American culture of the late 18th and 19th centuries may be visible in the archaeological record. My premise is that domestic sites of known Black occupancy will reveal patterns of material culture distinctive of Afro-American behavior. Attention is focused upon the habitation site of Lucy Foster, a freed Black woman who lived in Andover, Massachusetts during the early-mid-19th century.

Lucy Foster

Whether Lucy was African or American-born is uncertain. In an article on the history of Andover which appeared in *The Andover Advertiser*, August 29, 1863, Alfred Poor writes that "... she [Lucy] was a dau. of a slave in Boston, and was given to Mrs. C. [Chandler] when she [Mrs. Chandler] was the wife of Job Foster ..." (p. 2).

Little documentary information about Lucy is available. Glimpses of her life, however, are provided in the recorded affairs of Hannah Foster Chandler, her first husband Job Foster, and her second husband Philemon Chandler.

Job Foster, a well-to-do yeoman farmer in Andover (ECPR),[2] married Hannah Ford of Wilmington, Massachusetts on March 27, 1760. They resided in Andover where Job presumably continued to farm. When Lucy entered the Foster household is unknown, but she was present at least by 1771, since in July of that year she bore a daughter "given" to Job. The following entry appears in the records of the Andover South Parish Congregational Church: "July 14, 1771, Sarah, a child given to Job Foster and Lucy, a Negro, Child was baptized" (SPCR).[3]

Lucy was probably a servant in the Foster household. By the 18th century it was common throughout New England, and the North in general, for slaves to be used as domestics (Bailey 1880; Greene 1928). Females were cooks, laundresses, maids, and general household workers (Greene 1974: 110). Lucy probably served in such roles both before and after she gained her freedom, most likely in 1780 when Massachusetts slaves were emancipated.[4] Indeed, Lucy remained with the Fosters until Job died in 1782, and also stayed in Hannah's service until the latter's death in 1812 (ECPR).

Shortly after Job Foster's death Hannah remarried. Her second husband, Philemon Chandler, was also a well-to-do yeoman farmer in Andover (ECPR). The marriage occurred on February 2, 1789 (SPCR).

Exactly when or how Hannah and Philemon met is unclear, but both served as appraisers of Job's estate. John Abbot Jr., Joseph Ballard, Philemon Chandler, and Hannah Foster, administrator of the estate, appraised Job's real and personal property at £1046 17 04 (ECPR). But, on March 31, 1785, Joseph Foster, a son of Job and Hannah, complained to the probate court that substantial personal property had been omitted from his father's probate inventory (ECPR). Benjamin Greenleaf, judge of probate for Essex County, ordered the appraisers to reevaluate the deceased's moveables. On July 29, 1785, John Abbot Jr., Philemon Chandler, and Hannah submitted an addendum to Job's inventory which included additional personal property valued at £49 06 04 (ECPR).

Since Job died intestate and the documents of administration of his personal property have not survived, it is uncertain what percentage of his moveables was awarded to Hannah. With respect to the real estate, however, she received one third of all her late husband's holdings. Greenleaf appointed a committee of Andover freeholders "... to divide and set off by metes and bounds, one third part ... of all the real estate of Mr. Job Foster, yeoman, unto his wido Mrs. Hannah Foster for her use and improvement during her natural life" (ECPR). The committee recommended, and the court approved that Hannah be given certain tracts of land plus "... the east end of the dwelling house [Job's] from the top to the bottom as far as the middle of the chimney together with the south half of the cellar" (ECPR).

Hannah, attended by Lucy, probably remained in Job's house until 1789.

At this time she remarried, and, along with Lucy, moved to the Chandler homestead.

Two events marked Lucy's stay in the Chandler home: 1) "On Oct. 20, 1792, bapt. Peter, son of Lucy Foster, negro woman," and 2) on September 22, 1793, Lucy was admitted to the South Parish Church on profession of faith (SPCR). The father of Lucy's son is unknown as is her role in the Chandler household. What is certain, however, is that by 1800 both Hannah and Lucy no longer resided in Philemon's house. In recognition of kindness shown him in his later years, Philemon bequeathed Hannah $610.16, plus flax, wool, soap, cyder, apples, and the right to remain in his dwelling house for one year after his death (ECPR). He died on October 7, 1799 (SPCR).

By 1800, then, it is probable that Hannah and Lucy were again living on the Foster homestead. Hannah died on December 25, 1812, and the real estate mentioned both in her will and probate inventory clearly indicates that, at least at the time of her death, she was residing in her first husband's house (ECPR). Moreover, these documents reveal Hannah's beneficent feelings toward Lucy. In the first item of her will, Hannah writes, "I give and bequeath to Lucy Foster, the Black girl who lives with me . . . one cow, I also give to said Lucy one acre of land . . . [boundaries are given] " (ECPR). Here Lucy built a cottage in which she lived the remainder of her life.

In the 1863 newspaper article mentioned above, Alfred Poor gives the only known description of Lucy's dwelling place.

> When we get nearly over the plain we pass by the road which leads through the woods over the Chandler Bridge and the river street, and as we leave the plain, a sand bank called Black Lucy's garden, so named because a colored woman once had a cottage between this and the meadow, on an acre of land that was bequeathed to her by wid. Chandler. Capt. Joshua Ballard, with about $150 of her [Lucy's] own money, together with some more contributed by her friends, built her cot. about 1815, in which she lived about 30 years . . . (p. 2).

Poor's account is corroborated by primary information. First, Hannah's will, executed by Joshua Ballard, indicates that Lucy was given the acre of land (ECPR). Second, the $150 of "her own money" used to build her cottage probably is accounted for in the administration of Hannah's estate. The largest note paid from the estate is $126.15 to Lucy Foster (ECPR). And third, that Lucy occupied the cottage for about thirty years is supported by the fact that she died in 1845, age eighty-eight, just thirty years after the dwelling was built (SPCR).

How Lucy supported herself during the thirty years she lived in the cottage is uncertain. Although fifty-eight years of age by 1815, she may have continued as a servant, doing chores for local Andover families. Hannah's death, however,

Table 1. Lucy Foster's annual dole from the fund for the relief of indigent persons in the South Parish Congregational Church, Andover, Massachusetts

Year	Amount of annual dole
1813-21	$1.00 (per year)
1822-23	1.50 (per year)
1824-25	2.00 (per year)
1826	3.00
1827	1.50
1828	2.00
1829	no records
1830-35	2.50 (per year)
1836	3.00
1837-38	5.00 (per year)
1839-45	4.00 (per year

left her economically impoverished. Lucy's indigence is demonstrated by the dole she received from the South Parish Church. Immediately after Hannah's death, Lucy is identified as needy, and remains one of the parish poor until her death (see Table 1). By 1844 her health is failing and her economic condition is desperate. The following information is taken from the accounts of the Overseers of the Poor:

> *January 1844*, an order to Joshua Ballard for supplies furnished Lucy Foster (state pauper) $23.42.
> *February 17, 1844*, an order to Dr. Daniel Wardwell for attendance on Lucy Foster $1.34.
> *October 7, 1844*, an order to Joshua Ballard for relief of Lucy Foster $21.61.
> *July 7, 1845*, an order to William Balduni for expenses for Lucy Foster $1.25.
> *November 4, 1845*, an order to Joshua Ballard for supplies to Lucy Foster $1.75.

In this last account Ballard obviously is being reimbursed for funds already spent, since Lucy died of asthma on November 1, 1845 (SPCR).

The Black Lucy's Garden site, so named from the reference in Poor's article, was identified and excavated by Adelaide and Ripley Bullen in 1943. The house does not survive, but excellent information in Hannah's will plus documents that describe other properties allowed the accurate location of Lucy's one acre (Bullen and Bullen 1945).

The house burned probably soon after Lucy's death, and there was no further occupation of the site. Excavation provided charred wood as well as ceramic wares manufactured no later than the mid-19th century (Baker 1978; Bullen and Bullen 1945). Based on the number of sherds, the ceramic assemblage includes 64 per cent pearlware, 17 per cent redware, 13 per cent creamware, 2 per cent Chinese porcelain, 1 per cent delft ware, 1 per cent jackfield ware, 1 per cent local stoneware, and 1 per cent hardwhite ware. Furthermore, the absence of ironstone, which first appears circa 1810 and continues through the 19th century (Godden 1971), is negative evidence supporting the mid-19th century as the time of final occupation.

Excavated features associated with Lucy's occupancy are the cellar of the house, a well, a dump, and a vegetable cellar (Bullen and Bullen 1945). Upon initial examination the cultural materials retrieved appear identical to those from Anglo-American sites. Yet, when compared to recent findings from other Afro-American sites, artifacts and features at Black Lucy's Garden are seen to fit patterns not previously observed on sites of Anglo-Americans.

Ceramics and faunal remains

In his excellent study of status differences among planters, overseers, and slaves at Cannon's Point Plantation in Georgia, John Otto (1975; 1977) demonstrated a significant correlation among social status, shape of ceramic vessels, and dietary habits.

With respect to items of ceramic tableware, Otto found that serving bowls constituted 44, 24, and 8 per cent of the total tableware on the slave, overseer, and planter sites, respectively. Conversely, he found that items of serving flatware (i.e., plates and soup-plates), comprised 49, 72, and 84 per cent of the total tableware from the slave, overseer, and planter sites, respectively (Otto 1977: 106). Ceramic items apparently were issued to both slaves and overseers by the planter family (Otto 1977: 100). Knowledge of the diet of the former probably influenced the items provided.

Documents indicate that both slaves and overseers ate pottages and liquid-based stews of meat and vegetables, while the planter family ate roast meats and vegetables prepared individually (Otto 1977: 104). The zooarchaeological data support the documentary information. Remains of cattle, sheep, and hogs from the planter's kitchen reveal saw marks indicative of purposeful butchering to produce roasts. At the slave and overseer sites none of the bones has saw marks. Instead, these remains are chopped and split open. The extent to which the planter family influenced the diet of the slaves and overseers is uncertain. Food may have been issued or purchased. Nevertheless, it is clear that the slaves and overseers ate stews from serving bowls, while the planter family ate roasts from flat tableware.

Although Black Lucy's Garden was occupied by a freed northern Black, striking similarities exist between the archaeological data from this site and that from the Cannon's Point slave site.

Table 2. Serving bowls and serving flatware in percentage of all tableware.

	Slave cabin Cannon's Point Plantation	Black Lucy's Garden	Parting Ways
Total tableware count	80	49	81
Serving bowls	44	41	53
Flatware	49	51	46
Other tableware shapes	7	8	1

The minimum number of reconstructed ceramic vessels from the Black Lucy site is 113 (Baker 1978). Of these there are forty-nine items of tableware. Following Otto (1977), tableware is divided into serving bowls, flatware, and other shapes (e.g., tureens, pitchers). This classification reveals twenty serving bowls, twenty-five flatware vessels, and four other tableware vessels. Thus, bowls represent 41 per cent of the total tableware, while flatware and other shapes comprise 51 and 8 per cent, respectively.

In terms of faunal remains, 82 per cent of the cattle, sheep, and hog remains is chopped and cleaved open, suggesting that stews, not roasts, are the main bill of fare.

The patterns of ceramic shapes and faunal remains observed at Cannon's Point and Black Lucy's Garden are repeated at the Parting Ways site. Excavated by James Deetz, Parting Ways is a late 18th and 19th century rural community of four families of freed slaves in Plymouth, Massachusetts (Deetz 1977). A count of the minimum number of ceramic vessels, reveals eighty-one items of tableware (Baker 1976). These include forty-three serving bowls, thirty-seven flatware vessels, and one pitcher. Serving bowls, flatware, and other shapes comprise 53, 46, and 1 per cent of the total tableware, respectively (see Table 2). Moreover, without exception all of the faunal remains from Parting Ways are chopped, not sawed (Deetz 1977: 152).

Although affiliation of the above patterns to African cultural elements is unclear, the presence of serving bowls exceeding 40 per cent of all tableware, plus chopped faunal remains approaching 100 per cent of all such remains, appear distinctive of Afro-American sites, both slave and free.

Architecture

Excavation at Parting Ways revealed at least three undisturbed architectural features—one cellar hole and two sets of footing stones—associated with the Black occupants. The consistent dimension of these units was 12 feet, and not the standard Ango-American 16 feet (Deetz 1977: 144-149).

The 12-foot dimension, as Deetz notes (1977: 150-151), assumes great significance in light of John Vlach's recent research on shotgun houses in the American South and in Haiti, and on West African house types. Vlach (1976; 1978) has identified the shotgun house as a legitimate Afro-American architectural form. This is especially important since architectural units at Parting Ways strongly resemble shotgun houses in both floor plan and dimension. The 12-foot module, then, may represent a distinctive Afro-American architectural tradition. If such a tradition existed, one might expect to observe its remains on sites of other Afro-Americans. Well within the 12-foot range is housing of freed slaves living in Charleston, South Carolina. The description below is taken from an article entitled "Freed Blacks in Charleston, S.C." which appeared in *The New York Tribune*, June 30, 1869:

> The door was less than 5 ft high and it was the only entrance for light. The room was about 10 ft square with an earth floor; there was a fireplace made of sticks and clay ... and there were three beds made box shape of boards (p. 2).

Lucy also lived in a small cottage. Its construction was probably influenced by her desires and tastes, as well as by the modest amount she had to spend. The humble quality of the dwelling is indicated by its absence from the 1830 map of Andover (Dorman 1830). As previously noted, Lucy's cottage burned soon after her death, and there was no further occupancy of the location of her dwelling. Excavation of the undisturbed cellar showed that it was approximately square. The sides varied from 10 feet 6 inches to 11 feet 6 inches, while the walls varied in thickness from 18 to 25 inches (Bullen and Bullen 1945). Lucy's cottage clearly fits the 12-foot pattern.

Conclusion

Two features make Black Lucy's Garden distinctive: 1) the site was occupied by an Afro-American, and 2) this individual was poor. Similarly, Parting Ways was occupied by needy Blacks (Deetz 1977: 140-142). The issue, then, is that the patterns visible in the archaeological record may be reflecting poverty and not the presence of Afro-Americans.

For example, as John Otto demonstrated, the same pattern of faunal remains and, to a lesser extent, of ceramic vessels was present at both plantation slave and overseer sites. Since the overseers were white but of modest economic means (Otto 1977: 92), as were the slaves, the similarities in faunal remains and ceramics at the slave and overseer sites may be a function of their shared economic condition.

Presently, 12-foot architectural units, ceramic serving bowls, and chopped faunal remains provide the clearest archaeological visibility of late 18th and 19th century Afro-Americans. Only research on sites of poor whites, however, will substantiate fully the interpretive value of these three types of data.

Notes

[1] This paper has benefited from comments by Kathleen J. Bragdon, Marley R. Brown III, Dwight B. Heath, and Robert L. Schuyler.

[2] *ECPR* is the abbreviation used for the Essex County, Massachusetts probate records, Salem, Massachusetts.

[3] *SPCR* is the abbreviation used for the South Parish Congregational Church Records, Andover, Massachusetts.

[4] During the first half of the 19th century many northern Blacks, although no longer slaves, remained as laborers and servants (Litwack 1961; Provine 1973).

Bibliography

Bailey, Sarah Loring
    1880 *Historical Sketches of Andover (Comprising the Present Towns of North Andover and Andover), Massachusetts,* Boston: Houghton, Mifflin and Co.

Baker, Vernon G.
    1976 Ceramics from Parting Ways. Unpublished manuscript. Copy on file, Plimoth Plantation Library, Plymouth, Massachusetts.
    1978 *Historical Archaeology at Black Lucy's Garden, Andover, Massachusetts: Ceramics from the Site of a 19th Century Afro-American.* Papers of the Robert S. Peabody Foundation for Archaeology, volume 8. Andover, Massachusetts.

Blassingame, John W.
    1972 *The Slave Community: Plantation Life in the Antebellum South.* New York: Oxford University Press.

Bullen, Adelaide K. and Ripley P. Bullen
    1945 Black Lucy's Garden. *Bulletin of the Massachusetts Archaeological Society* 6(2): 17-28.

Deetz, James
    1977 *In Small Things Forgotten: The Archeology of Early American Life.* New York: Doubleday.

Dorman, Moses Jr.
    1830 A Plan of Andover. Copy on file, Andover, Massachusetts Memorial Library.

Garrett, Romeo B.
    1966 African Survivals in American Culture. *The Journal of Negro History* 51(4): 239-245.

Godden, Geoffrey A.
   1971   *The Illustrated Guide to Mason's Patent Ironstone China.* London: Barriet and Jenkins.

Greene, Lorenzo J.
   1928   Slave-Holding New England and Its Awakening. *The Journal of Negro History* 13(4): 492-533.
   1974   *The Negro in Colonial New England.* New York: Atheneum. (first published, 1942. New York: Columbia University Press.)

Litwack, Leon F.
   1961   *North of Slavery.* Chicago: University of Chicago Press.

Lomax, Alan
   1970   The Homogeneity of African-Afro-American Musical Style. In Norman E. Whitten, Jr. and John F. Szwed, eds. pp. 181-201. *Afro-American Anthropology.* New York: Free Press.

Otto, John Solomon
   1975   Status Differences and the Archeological Record: A Comparison of Planter, Overseer, and Slave Sites from Cannon's Point Plantation (1794-1861), St. Simon's Island, Georgia. Ph.D. disseration, Department of Anthropology, University of Florida, Gainesville, University Microfilms, Ann Arbor, Michigan.
   1977   Artifacts and Status Differences: A Comparison of Ceramics from Planter, Overseer, and Slave Sites on an Antebellum Plantation. In Stanley South, ed. pp. 91-118. *Research Strategies in Historical Archeology.* New York: Academic Press.

Provine, Dorothy
   1973   The Economic Position of the Free Blacks in the District of Columbia 1800-1860. *The Journal of Negro History* 58(1): 61-72.

Vlach, John
   1976   The Shotgun House: An African Architectural Legacy. *Pioneer America* 8(1&2): 47-70.
   1978   *The Afro-American Tradition in Decorative Arts.* Cleveland: The Cleveland Museum of Art.

CHAPTER 4

Weeksville: The Archaeology of A Black Urban Community

SARAH T. BRIDGES
BERT SALWEN

In the fall of 1968, a small group of Black residents and college students in the Bedford-Stuyvesant section of Brooklyn, in New York City, sought to involve the school children of the community in a project to gather as much information as possible about the history of their neighborhood, once known as Weeksville. This interest was spurred by the students in a Pratt Institute extension course on Brooklyn neighborhoods. Through the cooperative efforts of the residents and several local colleges and public schools, "Project Weeksville" was launched. The project started its explorations of neighborhood history by directing small groups of school children and boy scouts, as well as adults, in searching maps, property records, census records, and eventually, the material remains, for all traces of their history (Gutman 1976; Robert Swan, personal communication).

At first, there was no known written information about Brooklyn's first organized Black community. Although the name Weeksville appeared on a few 19th century maps and was occasionally mentioned by some of the older residents, this once prosperous free Black settlement, which flourished between about 1830 and 1870, was not referred to in any formal historical works. There were some very general references in the municipal records to Black land ownership in Brooklyn during the 17th and 18th centuries and census statistics for the county which indicated that large numbers of Blacks resided in the area prior to 1800. However, there was no information about the individuals who founded and developed Weeksville, on the social and economic processes that influenced the nature, form and direction of the community, or on the changes in the community during its short existence and eventual incorporation into the larger Bedford-Stuyvesant and Brooklyn communities.

Through a small-scale program of archival research (Hightower 1969; Gutman 1976), some information was gathered about the primary buildings in the community. This received some local press coverage (Anonymous 1971) which attracted the attention and eventual participation of young social historians concerned with the collection of oral history and the study of land-use and settlement patterns within Weeksville (Robert Swan, personal communication). This interest in the physical exploration of the community, coupled with interviews with the senior residents of the neighborhood, soon lead to studies of the above ground material culture and a community-sponsored subsurface archaeological study of a city block where some of the residences of Weeksville once stood. From these multidisciplinary researches a tentative outline of the history of Weeksville began to emerge.

The first postcontact settlements in Brooklyn were made by the Dutch during the 1620s. In 1640, a colony of Quakers from Massachusetts settled in Gravesend under the protection of the Dutch government (French 1860: 366). Throughout New York, the institution of slavery was strongly condemned by the Quakers. In 1799, the New York State Legislature provided for emancipation in gradual stages. Later, as northern European and West Indian immigration added to the paid labor force, the economic pressure to end slave competition with free labor increased. In 1827, slavery in the State was prohibited.

The community of Weeksville appears to have been established at about the time of the abolition of slavery (Hightower 1969; Robert Swan, personal communication). The community was probably named after James Weeks, a freeman, who bought property in the border area of Brooklyn between Bedford, Stuyvesant Heights, Crown Heights, and Ocean Hill. Oral history, much of it collected by the late William Harley of the Society for the Preservation of Weeksville and Bedford-Stuyvesant History, has provided the basic information directly associated with Weeksville.

Although most of Brooklyn's gridded road system was mapped in the 1830s, when Brooklyn was incorporated as a city (French 1860: 367), the grid system streets in the Weeksville area were not actually laid out until the middle of the 19th century. The only roads in the community during its first period of settlement and growth were of colonial origin. The primary thoroughfare, running northwest to southeast, was Hunterfly Road. When the grid street system was established after the Civil War, an order "pursuant to Chapter 132 of the laws of 1835" provided that Hunterfly Road be closed as soon as the eastern portion of Fulton Avenue was fit to travel (National Register of Historic Places 1972). New streets were developed in Weeksville, including Troy Avenue and Dean Street. Thus the settlement pattern of Weeksville followed two distinct conformations. Prior to the mid-19th century, the primary route in the community was Hunterfly Road; by the latter part of the century, Hunterfly Road was closed to traffic and became a small alley diagonally cross-cut by the grid system along which new development took place. It is believed that no building took place on Hunterfly Road after the 1840s (National Register of Historic Places 1972).

There has been reference to the construction of a frame house on the Weeks property in about 1825 (Hightower 1969). However, more recent local research indicates that Weeks purchased the parcel of land, presumably from the Lefferts family of Brooklyn, somewhat later, during the early 1830s; no single structure can be attributed to Weeks prior to that time (Robert Swan, personal communication; see also Maynard 1973: 28-29). Census and map research indicated that the community grew relatively rapidly between the 1830s and 1860s, supporting as many as thirty families in the vicinity of the Weeks property. A 19th century guidebook reveals that Weeksville was on the corner of the Lefferts' Brooklyn property (Maynard 1973: 29).

While the dates of construction of the community buildings have not been precisely determined, Perris's atlas of Brooklyn, dated 1855, shows a number of frame and brick houses as well as larger community structures, including: Colored School No. 2, later changed to P.S. 68; the Howard Colored Orphans Asylum; the Zion Home for Colored Aged; the African Civilization Society (an expression of early awareness of the need to identify and preserve the community's heritage); the Weeksville Baptist Church, later known as Berean Baptist Church; and the Bethel Tabernacle African Methodist Episcopal Church, built in 1847 and still on its original site. In addition, the Citizens Union Cemetery, just outside the boundary of the settlement, served the community. During searches through the attics of community dwellings, a copy of the constitution and bylaws of the Benevolent Daughters of Esther Association was discovered. This self-help organization was formed at a time when Blacks could get no commercial insurance coverage. The constitution was adopted in 1839 and printed by a local Black printer in 1853 (Maynard 1973: 30).

The draft riots of 1863 in New York and Brooklyn inaugurated a period of relatively rapid population growth in Weeksville. As Black families were driven out of their homes, they took refuge in Weeksville, among other places, to protect themselves from White rioters. One account, found during research in the Schomburg Collection of the New York Public Library, describes the assistance given to these refugees by the people of Weeksville. The account, by Wm. W. Wickes and R. P. Buck, dated September 14, 1863, states that several hundred individuals from surrounding areas were taken in and protected at considerable expense. Some of the refugees became permanent residents of the community.

However, by 1873, the *Brooklyn Eagle* of July 30 reported the gradual displacement of the Black population as New York City expanded and speculators acquired the land for development. Some of the Blacks were forced to relocate farther to the east. By the end of the 19th century, little was left of Weeksville as a community. The residents were assimilated into Brooklyn neighborhoods, and the name Weeksville was no longer used (Maynard 1973: 9). The material evidence of the community was dispersed and the area lost its former unique identity. Buildings were demolished; in 1946, the orphanage and elementary school were torn down to make room for a bus repair depot, and soon afterwards many of the residences were abandoned and demolished.

In 1968, under the Model Cities program, the City of New York proposed to demolish a full block of the old wooden structures located adjacent to the intersection at which stood many of the larger community buildings referred to above, to make room for low-income housing. Some recognized the potential loss of important historic resources, but, because the general preservation philosophy of the day focussed on properties which held greater aesthetic value for the majority of the preservationists, and because of the felt community need for new housing, no great effort was made to preserve the buildings in place. Rather, James Hurley, an historian at the Brooklyn Historical Society who had been working with local youth groups on history projects and whose long-term interest in the history of this area had resulted in the accumulation of a body of data that served as the basis for continued research, worked with local individuals and groups to develop Project Weeksville.

This archaeological and historical research and salvage program was designed and initiated entirely by the community itself; only after its inception did it receive solicited and unsolicited assistance from local academic and research institutions. Much of the 1968 archaeological effort was "above ground." It involved the recovery of material remains and architectural fragments from buildings destined for demolition. Mr. Hurley, working under the sponsorship of the Bedford-Stuyvesant Youth-in-Action, together with William T. Harley, the community resident referred to above, guided the Neighborhood Youth Corps in this building-by-building search for historical artifacts. The collections were made in a somewhat unsystematic manner, though general proveniences were usually recorded. While this initial effort did not always provide the kinds of information needed for anthropological studies of settlement system and cultural process, it did substantially enrich the scant written and oral history of Weeksville, and it provided the impetus for the more extensive scholarly and preservation projects which followed.

In 1969, with added funding from the City University of New York, salvage excavations were begun within a 7000-square-foot area, a full city block in Bedford-Stuyvesant (bounded by Troy and Schenectady Avenues and Dean and Pacific Streets), where the center of Weeksville once stood. The block under investigation was within the area scheduled for urban redevelopment, and, with the exception of two small factories, had been cleared of all above ground structural features prior to the initiation of the archaeological excavations. Fieldwork was conducted under severe handicaps, often in locations immediately adjacent to the machines which were demolishing the remaining structures.

The field effort was supervised by Mr. Harley, with advice from Michael Cohn of the Brooklyn Childrens Museum. Mr. Hurley was overall project director. The field crew, made up of adult volunteers, Boy Scout Troop 342, and work-study students from New York City Community College, worked on Saturdays throughout the fall and following spring, in 25-foot-square excavation units. In June 1970, under a grant to New York City from the National Science

Foundation, Bert Salwen and Ann Ottesen, of the New York University Department of Anthropology, established a training program in field and laboratory methods for the remainder of the field project. At this time, an additional grid of 5-foot squares was superimposed on the still unexplored portion of the site. Attempts were made to excavate these squares in stratigraphic units, but it was reluctantly concluded that the heavy demolition machinery had already destroyed most, if not all, meaningful horizontal and vertical contexts.

Archaeological research in urban settings often takes place under conditions unfavorable for maximum scientific control. This was particularly true prior to the mid-1970s, when professional emphasis began to shift away from crisis-governed research executed in the throes of demolition or construction, and toward controlled exploration of archaeological sites well ahead of demolition operations. The constraints of the crisis approach are often painfully apparent in the deficiencies of the recovered data; yet, in some cases, these data may be the only remaining sources of information about some aspects of the development of cities. In such situations, it becomes essential to develop theoretical, methodological, and analytical techniques which will extract the maximum amount of historical and cultural information from the incomplete archaeological record. At Weeksville, more than the usual quota of urban archaeology problems were encountered, and the need to develop appropriate analytical methods was particularly apparent.

The analysis of the Weeksville materials was performed by Sarah Bridges, of New York University, who worked under the general supervision of Professor Salwen. The ceramic specimens were chosen for the first full scale analytical treatment, first, because the majority of the sherds were from household tableware or utility pieces and thus directly associated with the daily activities of a representative sample of the members of the community; second, because some of the ceramic specimens could be reliably dated with relative ease; and, finally, because the ceramic assemblage was far larger than any of the other material categories in the collection.

Initially, all of the ceramic groups were listed according to gross horizontal provenience, but this exercise demonstrated clearly what had already been indicated by the fieldwork—there were no significant relationships between spatial distributions and artifact classes (Salwen and Bridges 1974: Table I). Hence, because of the mixed nature of the deposits at the site, it was necessary to view all of the archaeological specimens as comprising a single unit, essentially an undifferentiated surface collection. Conclusions concerning both chronology and culture would have to be based on the analysis of the formal attributes of the specimens themselves, supplemented by tentative correlations with oral and written historical data.

The 2,852 ceramic specimens were grouped according to their formal attributes. Ninety classes of specimens were defined (e.g.: buff earthenware; pearlware with blue, hand-painted "feather" edge; white salt-glazed stoneware;

Table 1. Quantitative differences in characteristics of ceramic groups from different time ranges

	Function		Place of Manufacture			Paste		
	Table-ware	Kitchen & misc.	Domestic	Imported	Unknown	Porcelain	Semi-porcelain	Pottery
1790-1835 Total: 69	69 100%	0 00%	0 00%	69 100%	0 00%	27 39.13%	0 00%	42 60.87%
1835-1875 Total: 710	306 43.10%	404 56.90%	417 58.73%	252 35.49%	41 5.78%	242 34.08%	45 6.34%	423 59.58%
1875-1900 Total: 1,235	1,000 80.97%	235 19.03%	297 24.05%	46 3.72%	892 72.23%	72 5.82%	65 5.26%	1,098 88.91%
1900-1969 Total: 523	508 97.13%	15 2.87%	19 3.63%	26 4.97%	478 91.40%	103 19.69%	16 3.06%	404 77.25%

Not included: 315 pieces unidentifiable as to these traits
Total ceramic sample 2,852 sherds
Source: Salwen and Bridges 1974: 19

undecorated ironstone, etc.). When these classes were arranged in chronological order, according to the time-span during which each was believed to have been manufactured, four clusters of manufacturing date ranges emerged. While the dates of manufacture of different classes of ceramics frequently overlapped, thus preventing the delineation of clear-cut boundaries between "periods," there were sufficiently distinct patterns of abandonment of old wares and introduction of new to suggest that these time ranges possessed some objective reality. To permit sociocultural interpretations, it was also necessary to assume that specimens whose dates of manufacture clustered chronologically were probably used contemporaneously by the inhabitants of Weeksville.

Based on these assumptions, it was possible to examine the quantitative differences in distributions of ceramic attributes within each of the four chronological periods, 1790-1835, 1835-1875, 1875-1900, and 1900-1969. Each group varied from the others in terms of material, locus of manufacture, and function, probably reflecting both changing ceramic technology and changes in cultural preferences over time (Table 1).

Because both the original collecting procedures and the assumptions made during analysis probably introduced unidentified errors, of unknown magnitudes, no attempts were made to separate the effects of technological changes in the North American ceramic industry from those of local shifts in preference, or to develop causal explanations for differences in relative frequencies among the ceramic assemblages from different "periods." Rather, simple correlations were described and tentative hypotheses were posed.

1790-1835

Only 2.4 per cent of the total ceramic collection falls into this temporal unit. Specimens include chinese export porcelain (Canton ware), pearlware, and imported English stone china (Salwen and Bridges 1974: 20-21). All were manufactured prior to 1810 and were out of production prior to 1836. As a group, they may represent the earliest, pre-Weeksville, occupation of the locality. However, because all of these specimens are fine tableware, with no corresponding utilitarian kitchenware pieces represented, this may not be a representative cultural inventory, but rather, remnants of a few heirlooms that were actually in use at a later date.

1835-1875

This temporal unit corresponds, in general, to the time of the first major growth in the population of the Weeksville community, and this growth is reflected in the increased number and variety of ceramic wares. 24.9 per cent of the total collection is included in this unit, which contains thirteen categories of ceramics. Thirty-five per cent of the sherds were imported, and 95 per cent of the imported pieces were tableware fragments, reflecting the inability of American producers to successfully manufacture porcelain at this time (Noel-Hume 1970: 100), and also suggesting a relatively prosperous economy that could rely on imported materials. It is interesting to note that the sturdier ironstone pieces are much less frequent in this unit. The majority of the utilitarian stoneware items were domestically manufactured, reflecting a long term pattern of local production of household wares. In general, the pattern exhibited by the ceramics of this unit seems consistent with the picture of community prosperity and growth indicated by the documentary evidence for new and varied construction during this period.

1875-1900

The ceramics assignable to this temporal unit, constituting 43.3 per cent of the total Weeksville collection, reflect an increase in population and some major economic and technological shifts. Tableware predominates over utilitarian wares, and the majority of the tableware specimens are of heavy earthenware and stoneware (Salwen and Bridges 1974: 24-25). When identifiable as to place of origin, domestically produced sherds predominate over imported ones. These statistics reflect the increasingly successful attempts of American producers to imitate the products of European potters (Noel-Hume 1970: 131), and also suggest a shift in the economic status of the residents to one of less affluence. This was the period of land speculation, and dispersal of the Weeksville community, as the urban metropolitan region expanded into this part of Brooklyn.

1900-1969

The ceramics of this temporal unit, comprising only 18.3 per cent of the total collection, may reflect a sharp drop in residential population, the introduction of new non-ceramic materials for the manufacture of household items that were formerly made of ceramics, or the continued use of ceramic objects made in earlier periods. Places of manufacture cannot be determined for the majority of the specimens, but in the cases where this is possible, all but one-half of one per cent are domestically made, reflecting continuing improvement in domestic ceramic technology. The overall drop in the frequency of all ceramics may be associated with the gradual industrialization of the Weeksville area, and the concurrent absolute decrease in its residential population.

The analysis of the ceramic collection, considered in conjunction with oral and written history, has identified two aspects of change which appear to be reflected in the archaeological record: one concerns sociocultural and demographic changes within the Weeksville community itself; the other concerns the development of the North American ceramic manufacturing industry. We have attempted to delineate some of these broad patterns. Our formulations are based on study of the ceramic sample alone, and are, of course, preliminary and tentative.

While the results of the archaeological research program at Weeksville are not particularly profound by normal professional standards, this project has frequently been cited to show how interdisciplinary efforts which include archaelogical components can provide useful information about communities that are not well represented in traditional written histories. Such communities, composed of ethnic or economic populations which have not been accepted into the "mainstream," are often systematically underreported in the documentary and literary records, but are nonetheless important parts of most urban regions.

This study has also demonstrated that so-called "disturbed" loci in urban areas can provide useful archaeological information; in fact, the very disturbance of the site may be the archaeological record.

The archaeological and historical research program has had substantial effects within the modern Bedford-Stuyvesant community. As a direct result of this study, a strong, well-organized, and nationally recognized preservation movement has developed. The material culture of Weeksville has become as important a source of both history and community identity as are its oral and written traditions. In 1971, the Society for the Preservation of Weeksville and Bedford-Stuyvesant History received a State charter, and the last remaining cluster of 19th century houses on Hunterfly Road, already a New York City Landmark, was listed in the National Register of Historic Places in 1972. The involvement and support of the community was the key to the success of this non-traditional preservation program (see Fleming 1971 for a planner's view of this project).

Today, a housing project stands on the site of the archaeological project; it is called Weeksville Gardens. Nearby, a museum of Afro-American and Black history has been established in one of the original Weeksville houses. The heritage of Weeksville has become an integral part of the daily life of the modern Black community, bringing it a fuller awareness of the richness of its history.

Bibliography

Anonymous
    1873   *Brooklyn Eagle*, July 30: 1-2. Brooklyn.
    1971   Weeksville: A Treasure of Black History. *New York Post*. October 5: 2, 7. New York.

Fleming, Ronald Lee
    1971   After the Report, What?: the Uses of Historical Archaeology, A Planner's View. *Historical Archaeology* 5: 49-61. Lansing, Michigan.

French, J. H.
    1860   *Gazette of the State of New York.* Syracuse: R. P. Smith.

Gutman, Judith Mara
    1976   Uncovering a Long-Lost Village. *New York Times.* February 22: 31. New York.

Hightower, Charles
    1969   Lost Black Community. *Daily World.* July 19: 9. New York.

Maynard, Joan
    1973   Black Urban Culture. *Historic Preservation* 25(1): 28-30. Washington: National Trust for Historic Preservation.

National Register of Historic Places
    1972   Houses on Hunterfly Road (N.R.) District. Nomination on file at the National Register of Historic Places, Office of Archeology and Historic Preservation, Heritage Conservation and Recreation Service, U.S. Department of the Interior. Washington, D.C.

Noel-Hume, Ivor
    1970   *A Guide to the Artifacts of Colonial America.* New York: Alfred A. Knopf.

Salwen, Bert and Sarah Bridges
    1974   The Ceramics from the Weeksville Excavations, Brooklyn, New York. *Northeast Historical Archaeology* 3(1): 4-29. Rome, N.Y.: Council for Northeast Historical Archaeology.

CHAPTER 5

Sandy Ground: Archaeology of A 19th Century Oystering Village

ROBERT L. SCHUYLER

During the 19th century Blacks not only lived within the urban core of cities like New York but also in satellite communities that were economically dependent on the city. General suburban expansion in the 20th century has absorbed and in most cases, as at Weeksville in Brooklyn, destroyed such settlements. Unique in the New York City region in that it has survived to the present is Sandy Ground or Woodrow, a small village that formed a "tiny racial island" on Staten Island.

Although both slaves and free Blacks were an element in the Staten Island population during colonial times and continued to live there after emancipation in the early 19th century, the inhabitants of Sandy Ground were in part immigrants. The history of their community is directly tied to the rise, decline, reestablishment and final collapse of the oystering industry in New York harbor. During the 17th and 18th centuries the harbor was rich in native shellfish, but after the colonial period overexploitation forced a reestablishment of the shell beds by the transplantation of seed oysters from the Chesapeake Bay. Free Blacks, an important segment of the oystering community in Maryland and Virginia, also travelled on the schooners and sloops that carried seed oysters to New York. Because of intensifying persecution in their home states a number of Black families, primarily from Snowhill, Maryland, migrated to Staten Island where they joined with local residents to establish the Zion African Methodist Episcopal Church. By the early 1850's this church had become the center for a small settlement.

Sandy Ground, as this community came to be informally called, was situated on a high, sandy section of Staten Island that was within easy reach of the estuary of Lemon Creek at Princes Bay (Figure 1). This bay was an important center for oysterboats. Although the community experienced some early hard

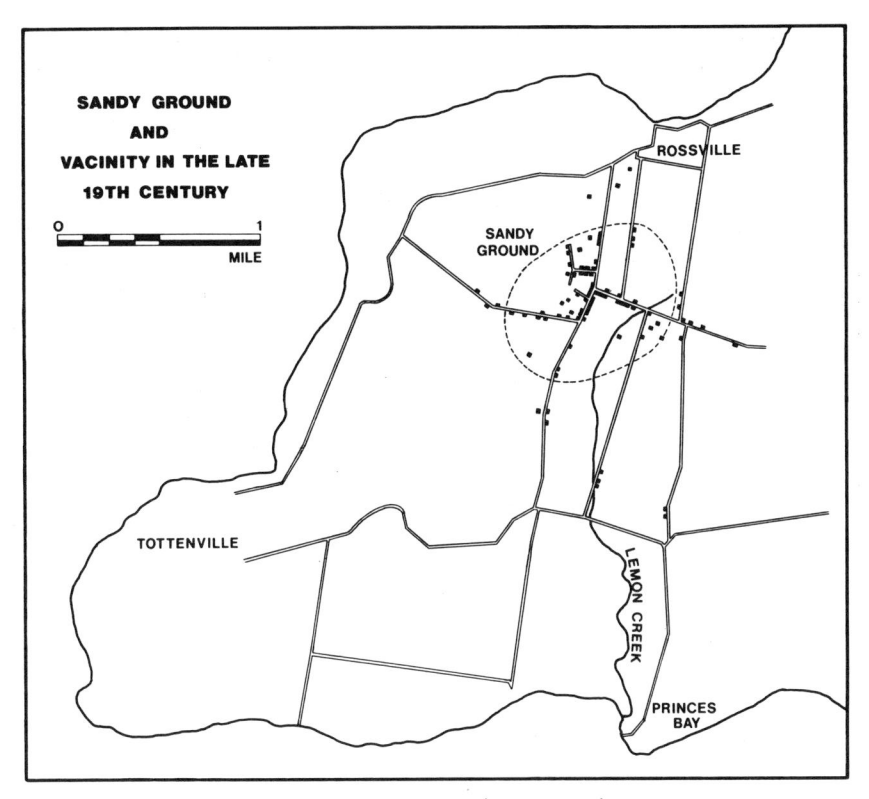

Figure 1. The boundary for Sandy Ground (dotted line) is approximate because the changing settlement patterns between 1850 and 1970 are still being researched. However, the community was always clearly set off by breaks between it and adjacent settlements at Rossville, Pleasant Plains-Princes Bay, and houses to the east and west. The roads and house symbols are not to scale.

years, it soon became a prosperous little oystering village (Wilkins, 1943a,b). By the time of the 1880 Federal Census about 140 Blacks in Sandy Ground clustered into thirty-eight residential units, intermixed with white families, that ranged from single old men or widows to large extended families. Twenty-two of these families had one or more members working on oyster boats, and some men owned their own sloops. The Landin brothers, for example, owned the *Fannie Fern* and employed a crew of ten. Other occupations such as blacksmithing also provided income and Sandy Ground was well known for its backyard horticulture, especially strawberries. Some families built and owned their own houses and, although they were not wealthy like some of the leading White oystermen who built mansions on the north end of the island, the village was economically stable and successful.

Sandy Ground's history, including the era of prosperity that lasted until after the turn of the century, is part of the history of New York City. Staten Island was and to some degree still is an isolated, rural section of the metropolitan zone. Nevertheless, Sandy Ground was always intimately tied into Manhattan. Its formation depended on the city and its history is one of a gradual intensification of this relationship. Initially the village was a specialized settlement that was rural in some aspects and urban-oriented in others. As the second half of the 19th century progressed an ironic dual relationship between Sandy Ground and New York emerged. The city established and strengthened the economic base of the community but simultaneously eroded that base. Industrial and human pollution began to effect the oyster beds in the late 19th century. Abruptly in 1916 the entire economic structure of Sandy Ground was broken when, following a series of typhoid cases, the Department of Health outlawed all oystering in the harbor. Sandy Ground went into decline and its residents were forced into the general labor market. Urbanization continued; air pollution from New Jersey industry eventually destroyed the possibility of local horticulture. In 1896 Staten Island was formally annexed by New York City and this suburbanization was greatly accelerated after 1964 when the Verrazano-Narrows Bridge opened the southern end of the island for development. The Westside Highway, constructed on Staten Island in the early 1970's, destroyed some of the remaining houses in Sandy Ground and recent housing projects have advanced so close that they are within view of the other side of Lemon Creek. Sandy Ground, although it is under extreme pressure in the late 1970's, is still a vital if small community centered around the AME Church.

Sandy Ground at the Turn of the Century

One of the best combined archaeological-documentary views of Sandy Ground is for 1900, near the end of its history as an oystering community. The most recent Federal Census tract is for that year and many of the archaeological features excavated to date produced materials dating from ca. 1890 to 1910.

Documentary Image

Although there are a number of unresolved problems in interpreting the various census data (Schuyler 1977), Sandy Ground at the turn of the century was still a stable community with a primary commitment to oystering. Within the core area of the settlement there were almost ninety individuals living in twenty-three residential units; twenty households with male heads with only three females in a similar position. Whether the noticeable difference between these data and those of 1880 imply a decline in population or rather are in part an artificial pattern created by the problems of setting boundaries and deciding

Table 1. Sandy Ground family structure in 1900

Type of Family	Number in that Category
Single Female	2
Husband-Wife	6
Mother-Daughter	1
Two Parents With Children	14

Number of Children in Each of These Units

1	(Daughter)	2	(1 D/1 S)
2	(Daughter, Son)	9	(4 D/5 S)
7	(5 D/2 S)	6	(4 D/2 S)
1	(Son)	1	(Son)
3	(2 D/1 Grand D)	2	(Sons)
1	(Daughter)	2	(D/1 adopted)
2	(1 D/1 S)	1	(Grand Daughter)

which Blacks were Sandy Grounders in the censuses, is not clear. The enumerator for the 1900 Census had penciled in "Sandy Ground" for a certain segment of the tallys (which in the main I am accepting) but this designation may be too limited. The age ranges (39 individuals between 0 and 20 years; 29 between 21 and 50; 17 between 51 and 90) seem normal, but there may be indications, including the possible population decline and a lack of younger working males, for the initiation of the economic strains that would lead to financial collapse fifteen years in the future.

Family size ranged from a single parent with one child to large families with seven or eight children (Table 1). Oystering was the primary activity of male heads of households with an absolute correlation between this activty and Blacks. Although White oystermen must have still been active on Staten Island they were not to be found in the immediate Sandy Ground area. Local White occupations ranged much wider including farming, shop keeping, factory (Dental Works in Princes Bay) work and other trades. Thirteen Black heads of households were oystermen with the remainder scattered in farming, general laboring, scavenging and religious ministration. There is no strong involvement of Blacks in farming but this would not exclude secondary activities such as horticulture or blacksmithing.

As almost half of the families owned their homes the community seems to have maintained its former success. Most of the oystermen, however, are listed as suffering three or four months of unemployment but this break is expectable in a seasonal trade.

Since Sandy Ground was a half century old in 1900 it is not surprising that most members of the community are listed as native New Yorkers. The

Chesapeake element, nevertheless, is still quite evident. A breakdown for heads of households and spouses is

New York	20
Maryland	7
Virginia	7
District of Columbia	1
North Carolina	1
New Jersey	1
Kentucky	1

A majority of oystermen, excluding younger sons born on Staten Island, were from the Chesapeake area. Several of the documented migrant families, like the Landins and Purnells, were still residents along with some early native Staten Island families like the Henrys.

In 1900 Sandy Ground was a specialized and discrete community focused on its church. It was economically viable and linked to the urban core to the North. Its Black oystermen were certainly tied directly to their markets in Manhattan. Yet this unique village, in its turn of the century state, had less than two decades remaining before the end of its traditional way of life.

Archaeological Image

Sandy Ground is a living community but it has an accessible, rich archaeological record. In 1963 a major fire on Staten Island destroyed several Sandy Ground structures, adding foundation ruins to those created by gradual abandonment. Between 1971 and 1973 (and again in the summer of 1979) survey and excavation of house sites and local, primarily late 19th century, dumps produced a series of assemblages that are being analyzed at CCNY (Schuyler 1974).

At the turn of the century Sandy Ground was still successfully adapted to the oyster industry with economic collapse a few years in the future. Two dumps (features 4 and 120), which were excavated in 1972 and 1973, present a replicated image of the place Sandy Ground occupied in metropolitan, regional, national and international trade networks. Both dumps are domestic, being composed of discarded bottles and other glass containers, ceramics, some metal objects and faunal remains including oyster shells. Chronologically they are roughly contemporary (ca. 1890-1905 or 1910) but are from separate areas of the site and thus represent different families. Whether these families were White or Black is not completely clear. Feature 4 was deposited in a natural depression opposite from two houses occupied by Blacks, while feature 120 could have come from a number of houses. A specific item from Feature 4, within the census context of only Black oystermen being in the area at this time, strongly implies an association with Blacks. A small, clear glass bottle (Cat. No. 4.15.33) bears the inscription "F. A. Shipley Central Pharmacy Seaford, Del." The Shipley Pharmacy was in operation between 1891 and 1909 and Seaford is not far from Snowhill, Maryland. In fact, Seaford was itself deeply involved in the Chesapeake oystering industry at the turn of the century.

Glass containers, such as this medicine bottle, are an important source of economic and behavioral information as they frequently have embossed inscriptions and logos (Figure 2). Contents, the company name (sometimes of both the maker and user of the bottle), and the geographical source are frequently given. The 4.15.33 specimen, for example, contained medicine, was from Delaware, and the bottle itself was made by the Whitall Tatum Company whose initials (W.T. & Co.) appear on its base. This company was a major bottle producer located in Millville, New Jersey.

When a tabulation of contents and provenience data, which is almost identical for both dumps, is compiled an image of the place Sandy Ground occupied in the trade networks operating in the metropolitan area at the turn of the century is created. The major categories represented are beverages (especially soda pop and beer), food, medicine and more exotic items such as perfumes and imported liquors. Soda pop even derives its name from this era when the Hutchinson stopper (ca. 1879-1915), consisting of a rubber gasket on a heavy wire loop, was opened by being forced down into the bottle. Escape of carbonation caused a distinctive "pop." It was only in the 20th century that the "crown top" replaced such cumbersome devices. Medicines for humans — "BUMSTEAD'S WORM SYRUP ONE BOTTLE HAS KILLED 100 WORMS/CHILDREN CRY FOR MORE/JUST TRY IT/PHILADA." — and animals represent, in turn, the great patent medicine hoax that was not to fall until the Pure Food and Drug Act of 1906.

Distributional patterns disclose a tight clustering around the metropolitan area for each feature (Figure 3). One bottle — "DALLEY'S CALVANIC HORSE SALVE/THE GREAT HOOF OINTMENT" — symbolizes that these deposits date just before the opening of the second phase of the Industrial Revolution when internal combustion and electronics were to revolutionize transportation, communication and most aspects of modern society. These are the very factors that are presently endangering the continued existence of Sandy Ground. Staten Island in 1900 was somewhat archaic in that it was totally dependent on water transportation. The first direct link to New Jersey or New York was not completed until the Outerbridge Crossing and the Goethals Bridge was opened in 1928. All goods and people moved in and out of the island by ferry or sloop.

A detailed tabulation of the two dump assemblages produces a well defined pattern (Table 2). Out of a total of 191 specimens only five bottles come from outside of the Middle Atlantic-Northeastern region. Of the 186 bottles that fall within this region nearly 78 per cent cluster within a tight 20 to 25 mile radius from Sandy Ground. A potential circle extending out from the site is not

54 / ROBERT L. SCHUYLER

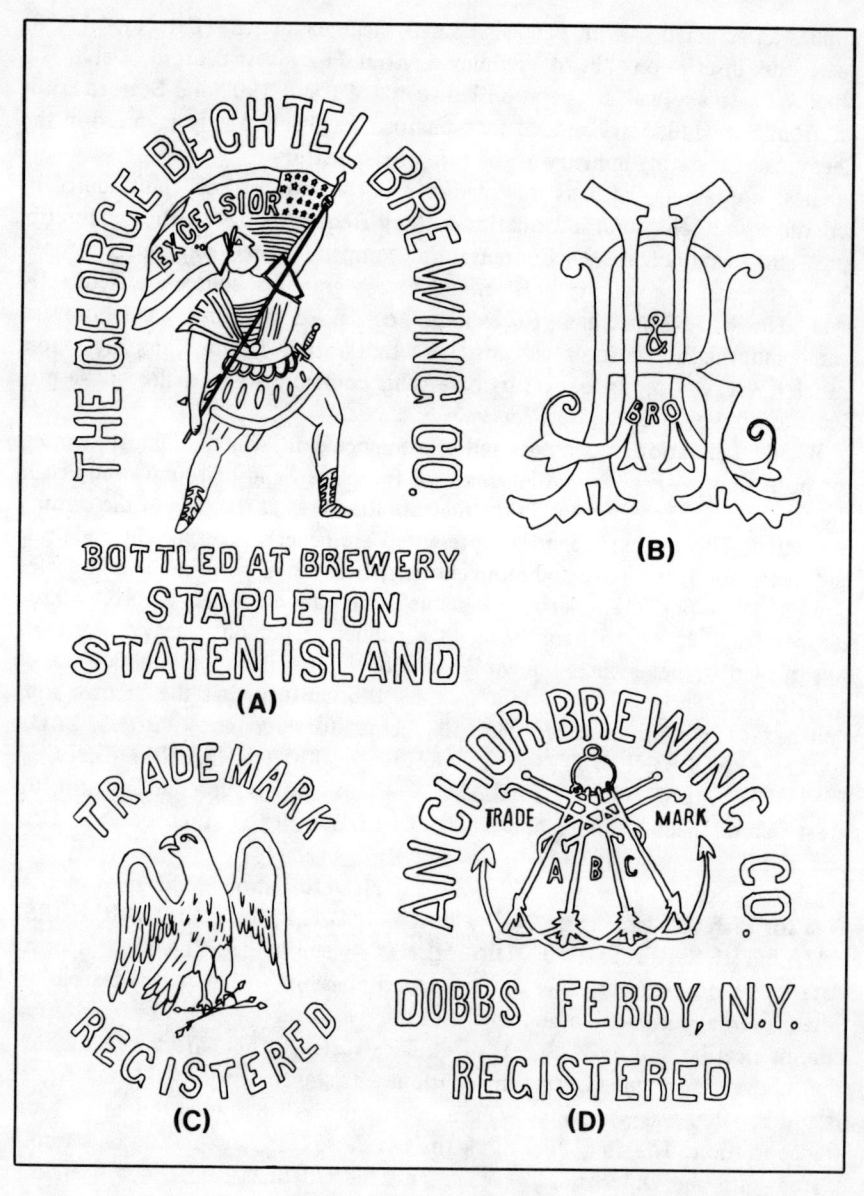

Figure 2. Examples of logos on bottles from Features 4 and 120

(Key to Figure 2 is on page 55)

complete as only one side of New York harbor is involved, with Long Island (particularly Brooklyn) have no representation. Actually the pattern is half an ellipse with one node being Staten Island itself (68 specimens), the other New York (56 specimens from southern Manhattan). A thin scatter of twenty specimens connect these two areas of concentration by an arc along the New Jersey shore. The fact that this tight pattern is, with some variation, the same for both Features 4 and 120 demonstrates that the two major orientations of Sandy Ground at the turn of the century were equally local and metropolitan. Another dump (Feature 5), which, unlike Features 4 and 120 which are surface deposits, is stratified, is clearly associated with a White Sandy Ground family and is in part contemporary (ca. 1890-1920) with Features 4 and 120. Analysis of its contents is in a preliminary stage. It will be significant if distribution patterns repeat or contrast with those outlined above. Perhaps the unique relationship of Black Sandy Grounders to Manhattan, via the oyster trade, is a factor behind the two-node pattern. Feature 5 may well reveal fewer bottles from New York City, relative to total count, and a more local orientation in all its contents.

Hopefully enough data can be derived from the 100 excavated dumps—most of which unfortunately are different from Features 4, 5 and 120 in that they have been badly disturbed by bottle collectors—to bracket the major transformation in this Afro-American community as it moved from economic stability to economic decline and collapse (1880-1920). A series of hypotheses on rapid

Key to Figure 2

(a) Several bottles from the George Bechtel Brewing Company of Stapleton were found in both Features 4 and 120. This brewery, one of several on Staten Island, was founded in 1853 by John Bechtel and passed on to his son, George Bechtel. It had gained such fame by the late 19th century that the Japanese ambassador, who visited New York in 1879, ordered 100,000 bottles for his homeland.

(b) Frank Hadkins moved this soft drink company from Perth Amboy, where his father had originally established it, to Tottenville where he ran it until 1872. In that year his son, Robert H. Hadkins took it over, being joined by his brother, Frank in 1887 ("R. H. HADKINS & BRO."). In 1889 the name was again changed, on the death of Robert, to the Hadkins Bottling Company. Several Hadkins bottles, bearing different logos, were recovered from Features 4 and 120.

(c) The eagle logo is of the "GEO. SPREITZER & CO. 1886 PATERSON, NEW JERSEY" (Cat. No. 4.18.6). On its base appears the initials GS&Co., an unidentified bottle producer.

(d) Anchor Brewing Company located at Dobbs Ferry, New York. This bottle (Cat. No. 4.4.4) is of clear glass and may be one of the more recent specimens. Unfortunately its top is broken off making it impossible to ascertain if it had an applied lip or a crown top (post-1903).

56 / ROBERT L. SCHUYLER

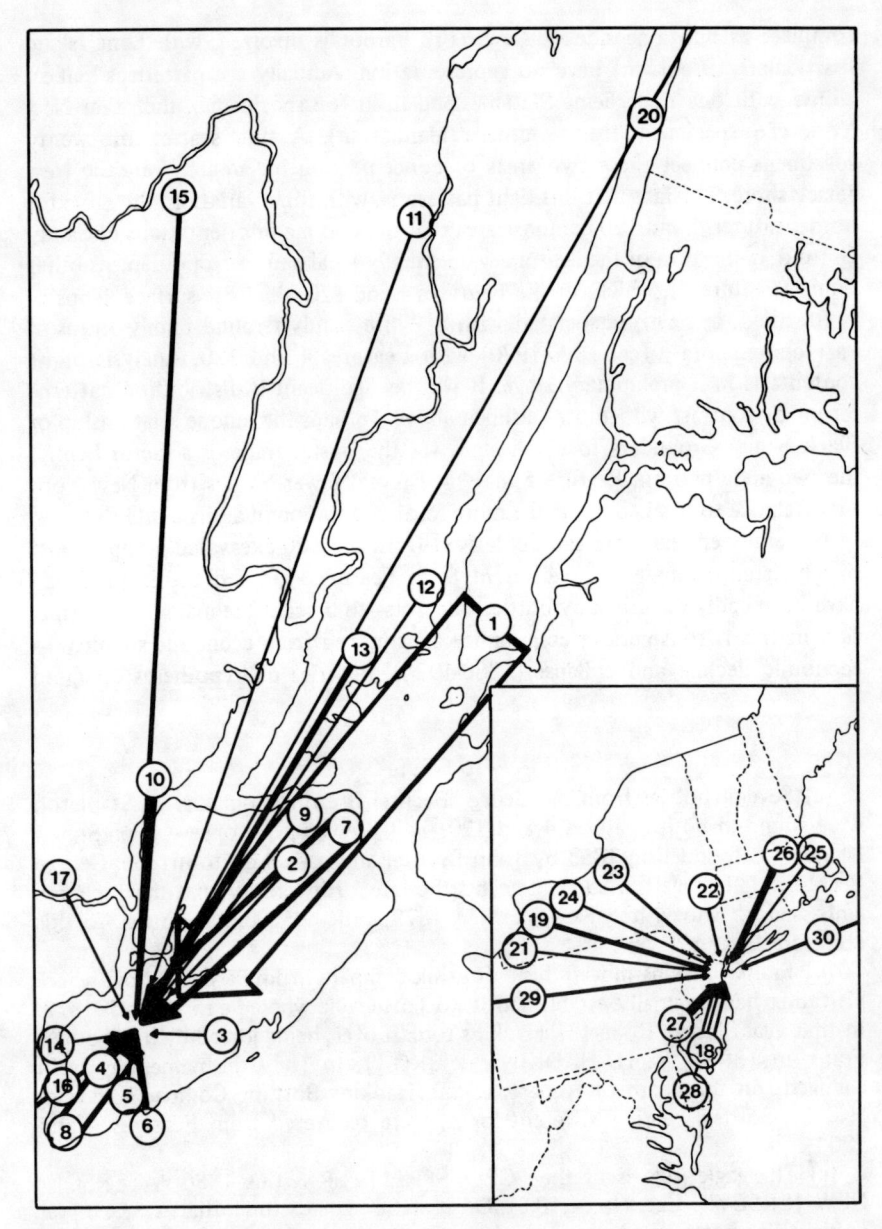

Figure 3. Flow of items into Sandy Ground at the turn of the century based on the glass containers from Features 4 and 120. The thickness of line is proportional to the number of items (see Table 2).

(Key to Figure 3 is on page 57)

economic change in an industrial setting have been discussed elsewhere (Schuyler 1974). Would the variety and quantity of goods being used by Black Sandy Grounders decrease, remain the same or increase? Would trade networks retrench, expand or remain static? It must be remembered that economic collapse, though it would reduce the standard of living, would also force the oystering families out of a specialized industry into the general labor market. It is known that after 1916 many Sandy Grounders were forced to look outside Staten Island for employment. Such movement might in turn make it possible for people to purchase a greater variety and range of goods.

Changes arising from economic perturbations would also alter demography, marriage and resident patterns and, eventually, all other aspects of culture. Sandy Ground, although unique in some of its characteristics, is also an example of the paradox of specialized satellite communities created by the city and then devoured by their creator.

Key to Figure 3

New York City	(1)	New York State	
Staten Island:		Buffalo	(19)
Concord	(2)	Dubbs Ferry	(20)
Eltingville	(3)	Dunkirk	(21)
Pleasant Plains	(4)	Hudson	(22)
Prince Bay	(5)	Oswego	(23)
Princes Bay	(6)	Rochester	(24)
Stapleton	(7)		
Tottenville	(8)	Northeast-Middle Atlantic	
West New Brighton	(9)	Region	
New Jersey		Boston	(25)
Elizabeth	(10)	Lowell	(26)
Hackensack	(11)	Philadelphia	(27)
Hoboken	(12)	Seaford, Dela.	(28)
Jersey City	(13)		
New Brunswick	(14)	Non-Regional	
Paterson	(15)	San Francisco	(29)
Perth Amboy	(16)	Europe	(30)
Rahway	(17)		
Millville	(18)		

58 / ROBERT L. SCHUYLER

Table 2. Sources for glass containers from Features 4 and 120

Map (Fig. 3) Number	Location	Number of Specimens Feature 4	Number of Specimens Feature 120
(1)	New York City	26	30
	Staten Island	21	47
(2)	Concord	1	—
(3)	Eltingville	1	—
(4)	Pleasant Plains	3	—
(5)	Prince Bay	2	—
(6)	Princes Bay	1	5
(7)	Stapleton	3	28
(8)	Tottenville	9	14
(9)	West New Brighton	1	—
	New Jersey	17	16
(10)	Elizabeth	—	5
(11)	Hackensack	1	—
(12)	Hoboken	1	—
(13)	Jersey City	1	4
(14)	New Brunswick	—	1
(15)	Paterson	1	2
(16)	Perth Amboy	1	2
(17)	Rahway	1	—
(18)	Millville	11[a]	2[a]
	New York	7	3
(19)	Buffalo	4	—
(20)	Dobbs Ferry	1	—
(21)	Dunkirk	—	1
(22)	Hudson	—	1
(23)	Oswego	2	—
(24)	Rochester	—	1
	Northeast — Middle Atlantic	8	12
(25)	Boston	1[a]	—
(26)	Lowell	3	4
(27)	Philadelphia	3	7
(28)	Seaford, Delaware	1	—
	Non-Regional	4	1
(29)	San Francisco, California	1	1
(30)	Europe	3	—
	London/Paris (?)	1	—
	Berlin	1	—
	Austro-Hungary	1	—

[a]Bottle producer rather than bottle user.

Future Research at Sandy Ground

Excavations between 1971 and 1973 explored two structures, one dating from the mid-19th century and the other from the late 19th century, and sampled or totally uncovered over 100 dumps. Most of these were surface or just subsurface deposits but one was a stratified pit over six feet deep. Presently there is a survey of the area in progress, under the direction of William Askins (CUNY), that is attempting to inventory all visible ruins and standing structures. This work is an initial step in an effort to have Sandy Ground designated as a historic zone which would offer it some protection from continuing encroachment by suburbia.

The pioneering work of Minna Wilkins in oral and documentary history is being updated and expanded by researchers at the Staten Island Institute of Arts and Sciences, under the supervision of Gail Schneider. Hopefully a culture history of Sandy Ground from 1850 to the 1970's based on archaeology, oral history and archival sources will be the final result.

Acknowledgments

Sections of this paper were previously published as *Bulletin* 69 of the New York Archaeological Association. All illustrations are by William Askins.

Bibliography

Schuyler, Robert L.
- 1974 Sandy Ground: Archaeological Sampling in a Black Community in Metropolitan New York. *Papers of the Conference on Historic Site Archaeology* 7(2) 12-52. University of South Carolina.
- 1977 The Spoken Word, the Written Word, Observed Behavior and Preserved Behavior: the Contexts Available to the Archaeologist. *Papers of the Conference on Historic Site Archaeology* 10 (2) 99-120. University of South Carolina.

United States Censuses
- 1880 *Tenth Census of the U.S.*, State of New York, County of Richmond, Townfield of Westfield, U.S. National Archives. (New York Public Library).
- 1900 *Twelfth Census of the U.S.*, State of New York, County of Richmond, U.S. National Archives and Record Center, Bayonne, New Jersey.

Wilkins, Minna C.
- 1943a Sandy Ground: A Tiny Racial Island. *The Staten Island Historian* 6 (1) 1-3; 7. Richmond Town, Staten Island.
    - b Sandy Ground: A Tiny Racial Island: Part II. *The Staten Island Historian* 6 (4) 25-26; 31-32.

CHAPTER 6

Skunk Hollow: A Preliminary Statement on Archaeological Investigations at a 19th Century Black Community

JOAN H. GEISMAR

Introduction

Located on the Palisades just south of the New York–New Jersey state line are the cellar holes, stone foundations, stone wall boundaries and road remnants defining the Skunk Hollow Site.[1] Research has revealed that this site represents the oldest and longest occupied segment of a 19th century, rural black community (ca. 1806-1905). Comprising ca. 115 acres, the ruins of approximately twenty structures are evident; a cemetery area is identified by a single blank grave marker and several ground depressions. Since the 1950's the site has been altered by the building of a major highway but, aside from the highway strip itself, it seems only minimally disturbed by this construction.

The terrain is composed of alternating hills and swamps and is crossed by streams (Figure 1). The topography appears unsuited to the large farms characteristic of a 19th century economy or the development associated with 20th century economics. This factor, and the eventual inclusion of the land into Palisades Interstate Park, has resulted in unusually good preservation for a long-abandoned 19th century community site.

Tax records, census manuscripts, deeds and a diary—plus oral histories—have disclosed that Skunk Hollow is historically interesting and presents a sharply defined cultural manifestation ideal for anthropological research. Since the community is defunct, the behavioral aspects of its lifeway are now retrievable only through analysis of the material remains of the culture—the resources of an archaeologist. Because it was inhabited by local freed slaves and several generations of their descendants, and because of its excellent preservation, information to be recovered from this site potentially relates to several disciplines. This potential includes applying a quantitative, comparative anthropological approach

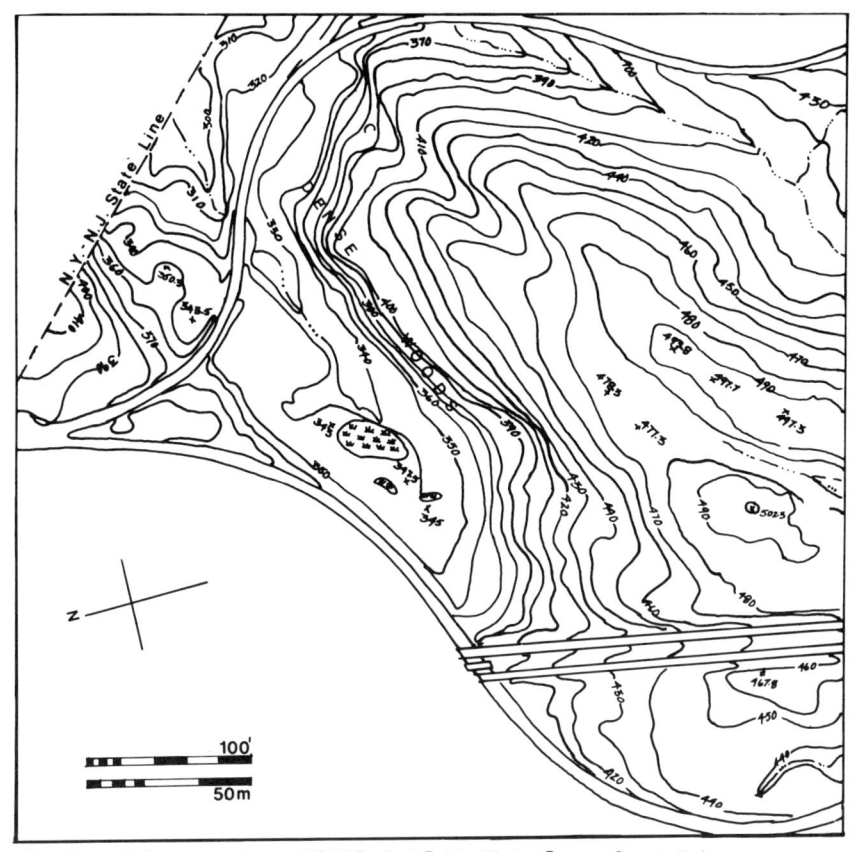

Figure 1. Skunk Hollow — contour map

to an historic archaeological site (South 1977: 1-45). Application of this approach to the analysis of historic sites shifts the focus from documentation alone to examination of complete cultural remains represented by the site (Schuyler 1972). This holistic approach also permits the testing of criteria proposed for archaeologically determining patterns of black ethnicity found at relevant 19th century house or community sites.

Based on the Parting Ways Site in Plymouth, Massachusetts, dwelling dimensions, settlement pattern and dietary refuse have been suggested as parameters of black ethnicity (Deetz 1977: 148-153). Recognizing that Skunk Hollow and

Parting ways are dissimilar in geographic location, dominant culture, size and economic status,[2] documented similarities validate comparison. These similarities include the contemporaneity of the sites and the known origin and ethnicity of their inhabitants.

In addition to Parting Ways, several sites suitable for comparative analysis with Skunk Hollow have been archaeologically investigated, making further intersite comparison feasible. These include the Black Lucy's Garden Site in Andover, Massachusetts (Bullen and Bullen 1945), Weeksville in Brooklyn, New York (Salwen and Bridges 1974), Sandy Ground on Staten Island, New York (Schuyler 1974) and the Cannon's Point Plantation Site in Georgia (Otto 1977).

At present, the reconstruction of historic and economic profiles for Skunk Hollow is almost complete. Therefore, a summary of this aspect of the investigation can be presented.

Historic and Economic Profiles for Skunk Hollow

Because the community was rural, and perhaps because it was composed of free blacks initially attempting to maintain a low profile (Calligaro 1967), primary documentation is somewhat fragmentary. Still, research has provided information with which to construct historic and economic profiles of the community.[3]

The first deed recorded to a free black in Skunk Hollow was to Jack Earnest, a man born a slave in an adjacent part of Rockland County in New York (Gesner 1841: 12-13). Dated January 7, 1806 (BCDB Y: 86-88), the deed predates formal emancipation in New York State by twenty-one years (McManus 1961: 26) and in New Jersey by forty-one years (Calligaro 1967: 170).

Although no deeds can be located for the years between 1806 and 1841, Skunk Hollow names appear on Federal census manuscripts for 1830 and 1840 and in Harrington Township tax records for 1813 and 1822. It may be that many eventual landholders in the community were living in the area at this time as tenants or squatters. Sometime between 1830 and 1840 two blacks who can later be identified as Skunk Hollow residents, and who may have been born in Virginia (FCHT 1860: 121), appear in the records, but for the most part the early inhabitants of the community appear to be local freed blacks. For a time succeeding generations continued to expand the land holdings and number of dwellings in the community. In addition, apparently prior to the Civil War, a Methodist Episcopal church was erected (BCDB B5: 144-147). Its minister, from whom the church land was bought, was an early and enduring resident of Skunk Hollow (BCTR 1822; SCHT 1885: 74). The deed to ". . . the Trustees of the Methodist Episcopal Church of Coulered (sic) People of the Township of Harrington . . ." indicates that this was the first church of this denomination in

Harrington Township specifically for blacks. Although there were other free black families living in the township, this community appears to be the only cluster of its kind throughout the area during the 19th century.

The economic status of Skunk Hollow as a community seems singular. From the scanty tax information available for Harrington Township in the 1800's—nine records for the years between 1802 and 1822; one for 1850 and one for 1854—it appears that the average Skunk Hollow tax was consistently higher than the average tax paid by other free blacks. In 1850 the average tax paid by Skunk Hollow residents slightly exceeded the average paid by other township taxpayers, white and black. Also, while free black females in the township in general were often listed on census manuscripts as engaged in service occupations such as laundress or servant, Skunk Hollow females were not working. At least this was true until 1905. On the other hand, the occupation listed for men in Skunk Hollow was consistently that of "laborer" or "day laborer"—the minister being the major exception. This remained the case throughout the 19th century even with increasing industrialization of the area. Yet one "laborer," a taxpayer as as early as 1822, owned approximately seven acres in Skunk Hollow. At his death in 1855 he was solvent enough to leave a will—albeit the only one recorded for a Skunk Hollow resident—and a relatively substantial inventory (BCRI Book G 1835: 51-52). Two-thirds of his land was divided equally between his five male and female children, one-third went to his widow (BCOCR Book G 1856: 48-49).

From this brief summary a picture emerges of Skunk Hollow residents as more affluent than their black counterparts in the township at large, but not affluent by white standards. This is true at least for the first seventy-five years of the community's development. After 1880 the records indicate a disintegrating economic situation.

Unemployment data found in the Federal census manuscripts for 1880 and 1900 mark a sharp increase in the percentage of unemployment in Skunk Hollow within this twenty year period. In 1880 Skunk Hollow unemployment was much less than for blacks in the township; by 1900 the percentages were equal. This rise in unemployment seems concommitant with population decline. By 1900 the black population in general had decreased sharply in Harrington Township (cf., FCHT 1880; SCHT 1895; FCHT 1900); a decline also occurred in Skunk Hollow. At its demographic peak, between 1870 and 1880, there were twelve active households in the community cluster. By 1885 the number had dropped to seven; by 1895, five; by 1900 and 1905, three; by 1915, none. The 1918 tax records for Alpine indicate that any Skunk Hollow land that had not been sold to speculators had been bought by the Borough of Alpine for back taxes (ATR 1918: 30-34).

The documented disintegration of Skunk Hollow as a functioning community was undoubtedly the result of many interrelated factors generated from both within and outside the community. As the 19th century progressed, and industrialization increased, the New York—New Jersey area in which the community was located became more developed and therefore less isolated. Steamboats in the late 1820's, the railroad in 1841 (Scott 1976: 15), and new roads increasingly tied the local economy to a larger economic sphere, including New York City and beyond (Scott 1976). With decreasing isolation the economy in the area became more dependent on the economic fluctuations in the world at large and personal contact with this world increased. For example, records indicate an increase over time in deeds to people from New York City while census manuscript data disclose an increase in European immigrant population.

In 1895 the community church was moved to Sparkill, New York (Pierson 1977: p. c.) and, as seen from the information given above, whether by choice or because of factors beyond the control of its inhabitants, Skunk Hollow ceased functioning as a community early in the 20th century. Population dispersal was mainly to nearby towns and villages where descendants of Skunk Hollow families are still to be found.

The Archaeology of Skunk Hollow

From 1975 to 1978 fieldwork at Skunk Hollow was carried out by members of the Columbia University Department of Anthropology Field School. Approximately thirty days were spent in excavation. In 1975 and 1976 work was completed on a cellar hole and associated features, including an outbuilding, a section of midden, and two adjacent, unidentified, rectangular stone-lined pits. Elsewhere at the site, what is believed to be the church foundation and an associated stone-lined pit or well and an unrelated outbuilding were excavated during the 1977 and 1978 field seasons (Figure 2).

The identification of a large stone foundation as the church is indicated archaeologically by the absence of a cellar hole, the paucity of domestic or "daily-living" artifacts and the profusion of architectural artifacts (e.g., window glass, nails and plaster in the artifact assemblage). Also, it appears to be the largest foundation at the site, ca. 20.5' (6.25 m) by 26' (7.87 m). Identification of this feature as the church is corroborated by the description of the land found in the church deed (BCDB B5: 145).

The distribution of architectural artifacts (see Figure 3)—a brick cluster on the east wall, and a stone footing centrally located outside the south wall (this is not shown in Figure 3)—and the location of the pit or well ca. 5' (1.5 m) beyond the western segment of the north wall, suggest the church structure and orientation. A windowed, wood building set on a stone foundation, with the door in the south wall and a chimney in the east wall, is implied.

To facilitate a comparative study of the site's features, a surface collection was made during the summer of 1978. Since analysis of material from Skunk Hollow is in a preliminary stage, it would be premature to undertake a detailed discussion of the artifacts or structures.

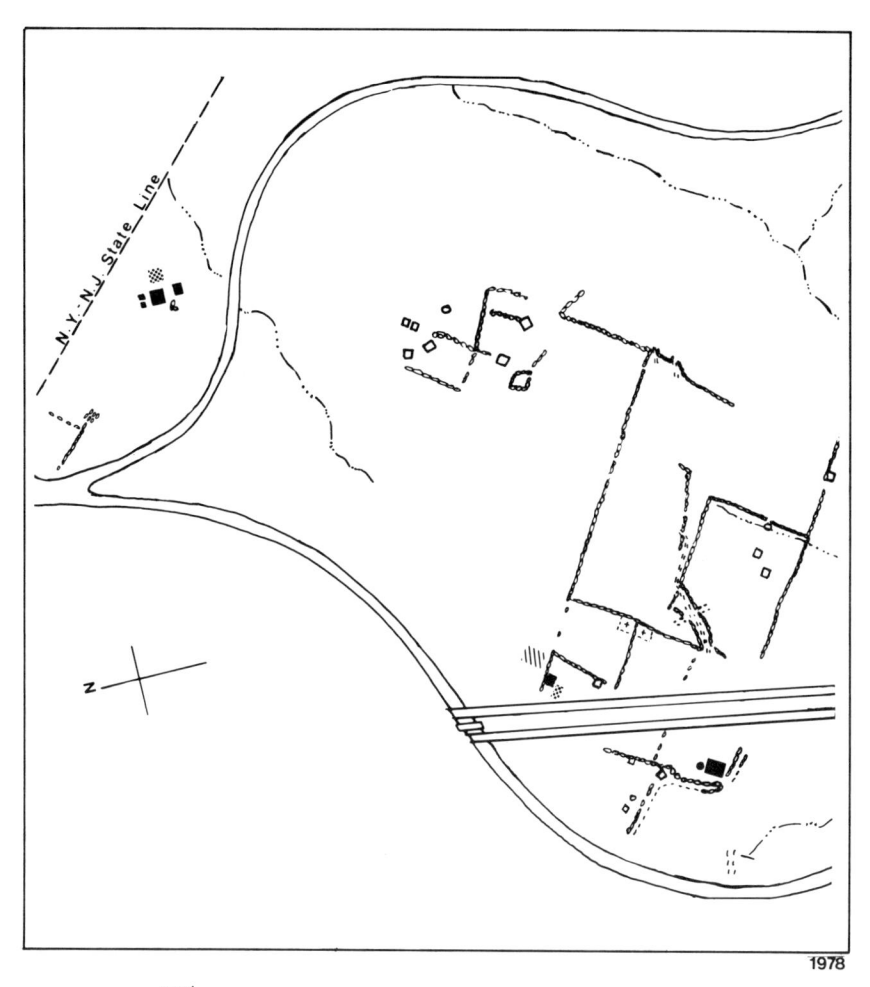

SKUNK HOLLOW / 65

1978

100'
50m

KEY
(features not to scale)
═ - modern road; ⁻⁻⁻⁻ - old road; ■ - excavated structure; □ - unexcavated structure;
⎯⎯ - brook; ∞ - stone wall; ⟨⁺⟩ - cemetery; ● - excavated feature (non-structure);
○ - unexcavated feature (non-structure); ▓ - excavated midden; ▨ - known midden
(unexcavated).

Figure 2. Skunk Hollow — feature map

66 / JOAN H. GEISMAR

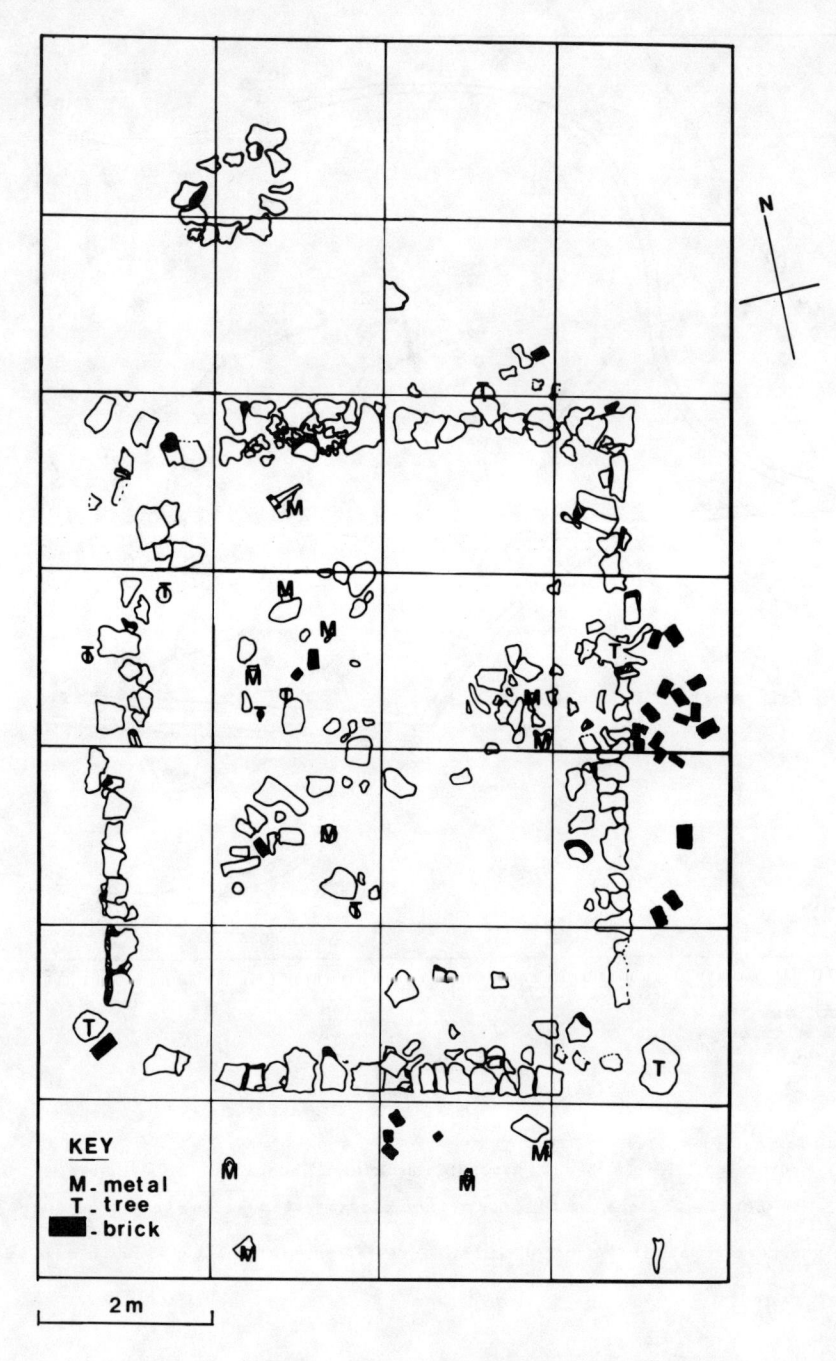

KEY
M - metal
T - tree
▬ - brick

2 m

Figure 3. Skunk Hollow Church — 1977

Conclusion

Although the archaeological investigation and analysis of Skunk Hollow is in its preliminary stages, it is possible to comment on the archaeological potential of the site.

Potentially the site will increase our understanding of culture patterning at 19th century black communities and house sites; its suitability to testing proposed criteria for archaeologically determining black ethnicity at such sites is evident. It is anticipated that at completion of the investigation of Skunk Hollow many aspects of culture patterning in the 19th century will be better understood. It is also expected that information garnered from this investigation will ultimately contribute to anthropology, archaeology, history and related disciplines.

Notes

[1] The name "Skunk Hollow" has been given to the site for this study. Locally it was referred to as "the Mountains," but oral history also acknowledges Skunk Hollow as a place name.

[2] New England was basically Anglo-American in culture while New York and New Jersey in the site area was populated by people of predominantly Dutch descent. Also, the community of Parting Ways consisted of four households, while at its demographic peak Skunk Hollow consisted of twelve. Finally, although it was marginal, Skunk Hollow appears economically independent in the 19th century while inhabitants of Parting Ways were under the guardianship of an Overseer of the Poor, the 19th century equivalent of welfare (Crosby n.d.).

[3] See Schuyler 1977 for discussion of this method.

Bibliography

Abbreviated References

ATR	Alpine Tax Records, Alpine Town Hall, Alpine, New Jersey.
BCDB	Bergen County Deed Book, County Clerk's Office, Hackensack, New Jersey.
BCOCR	Bergen County Orphans Court Records, County Clerk's Office, Hackensack, New Jersey.
BCRI	Bergen County Record of Inventories, County Clerk's Office, Hackensack, New Jersey.
BCTR	Bergen County Tax Rateables 1778-1822, The New Jersey Room, Fairleigh Dickinson University, Rutherford, New Jersey.
FCHT	Federal Census, Harrington Township.
SCHT	State Census, Harrington Township.

References

Bullen, A. K. and R. P. Bullen
   1945   Black Lucy's Garden. *Bulletin of the Massachusetts Archaeological Society* VI(2): 17-28.

Calligaro, Lee
   1967   The Negro's Legal Status in Pre-Civil War New Jersey. *The New Jersey Historical Society* LXXXV(3-4): 167-180.

Crosby, Connie
   n.d.   Report on Parting Ways, m.s.

Deetz, James
   1977   *In Small Things Forgotten.* New York: Doubleday.

Gesner, Nicholas
   n.d.   Unpublished Diaries, 1829-1850. Palisades: Palisades Free Library.

McManus, Edgar
   1961   Antislavery Legislation in New York. *The Journal of Negro History* XLVI(4): 207-216.

Otto, John Solomon
   1977   Artifacts and Status Differences—a Comparison of Ceramics from Planter, Overseer and Slave Sites on an Antebellum Plantation. In *Research Strategies in Historical Archaeology.* Stanley South, ed. pp. 91-118. New York: Academic Press, Inc.

Pierson, Frances
   1977   Personal Communication. New York: Piermont.

Salwen, Bert and Sarah Bridges
   1974   The Ceramics from the Weeksville Excavations, Brooklyn, New York. *Journal of the Council for Northeastern Archaeology.* Spring, 1974: 4-29.

Schuyler, Robert L.
   1975   The Written Word, the Spoken Word, Observed Behavior and Preserved Behavior: the Various Contexts Available to the Archaeologist. *Conference on Historic Site Archaeology, Papers* 10(2): 99-120.
   1974   Sandy Ground: Archaeological Sampling in a Black Community in Metropolitan New York. *Conference on Historic Site Archaeology, Papers* 7(2): 13-51.
   1972   Historical and Historic Sites Archaeology as Anthropology: Basic Definitions and Relationships. In *Contemporary Archaeology.* Mark P. Leone, ed. pp. 118-124. Carbondale and Edwardsville: Southern Illinois University Press.

Scott, John H.
   1976   The Slote, Piermont and the Erie Railroad. *South of the Mountains, Rockland County Historical Society* 20(3): 5-21.

South, Stanley
   1977   *Method and Theory in Historical Archaeology.* New York: Academic Press, Inc.

CHAPTER 7

The African Meeting House: The Center for the 19th Century Afro-American Community in Boston

BETH ANNE BOWER
BYRON RUSHING

For the past three years the Museum of Afro-American History has conducted an archaeological testing program at the African Meeting House.[1] The African Meeting House is located on Smith Court on the north slope of Beacon Hill, Boston, Massachusetts (see Figure 1). In the 19th century the church was a center for Afro-American religious, civic and educational activities. The building is presently being restored to its mid-19th century appearance for use by the museum. It was decided that archaeological investigation around the Meeting House might be able to fill some of the gaps in information concerning the original appearance of the church and its site, as well as the community the Meeting House served. Information on Afro-American communities in the 19th century is noticeably lacking in historical records. Little is known about the community on Beacon Hill: how the people lived, what they ate, and in what ways they were a part of the mainstream of American culture. It was our hope that excavation at the Meeting House would give us some insight into 19th century urban Afro-American culture.

The African Meeting House was built in 1806 by black craftsmen under the direction of Ward Jackson, master builder. It is a three story brick structure in the Federal style. Its design was probaby taken from Asher Benjamin's book *The American Builder's Companion* (1806). Materials from the West church of Boston, built in 1736 and torn down in 1805, were reused at the Meeting House. The original plan of the Meeting House had a basement containing two rooms at the south end for the pastor and a school room in the other half. Soon after it was finished the independent school for black children moved its quarters to the church. The second floor contained the main sanctuary and above this was the gallery. In around 1855 a major fund raising drive and revitalization movement was conducted to renovate the church building. The schoolroom, which

Figure 1. Historic photograph (ca. 1875) of the African Meeting House. (Courtesy of the Museum of Afro-American History, Boston, Massachusetts.)

had been in disuse for years after the Smith school was built, was reclaimed by the deacons of the church. Although its appearance was probably not altered radically, its function changed to that of a lecture hall or meeting room. A slate covered apse was added and the sanctuary and gallery were altered. In the late 19th century the building was renovated again. This work probably occurred after the building was acquired by the Congregation Libavitz in 1898. The basement was gutted and the floor deepened. Additional doors and windows were added on the basement level. The building remained this way until it was bought by the Museum of Afro-American History in 1972. The museum has decided that the exterior and upstairs interior of the church should be returned to its post-1855 appearance.

In the 18th and 19th centuries Boston had a large free black population. Many slaves were freed after the American Revolution and slavery was not widely practiced in Massachusetts after this time. In the late 18th century the Afro-American community lived in the north end in the area the whites called "Guinea Coast." In the early 19th century there was a move by some black leaders to relocate to the West end of Boston and the north slope of Beacon Hill, an area just being settled. When the first black church building, the African Meeting House, was built on Beacon Hill in 1806 this migration gained momentum.

Between 1800 and 1900 most of the Afro-Americans in Boston lived on the north slope of Beacon Hill. The population clustered on various streets and alleys around the African Meeting House. The neighborhood also had a white working class element until 1865 when black migration from the southern United States flooded Boston and made this area predominantly Afro-American. In the first half of the 19th century the majority of the Afro-Americans held service occupations: hairdressers, barbers, laundresses, waiters, clothiers, mariners and laborers (Boston Directory 1831). Many held jobs with the affluent white households on the south slope of Beacon Hill. A number of the residences were rented and were occupied by several households. Institutions were founded within the community for social, educational and charitable reasons. These included the African Society of Boston, the Garrison Juvenile Society, the Adelphic Union Library Association, and various benevolent societies.

The African Meeting House was constructed in 1806 with fund raising assistance from the First Baptist Church of Boston. Thomas Paul served as pastor from 1806-1829 and was considered one of the leaders of the Afro-American community. Just before Paul's resignation in 1829 for reasons of health, a controversy arose within the church membership which resulted in the secession in 1840 of the minister, George Black, and forty members of the congregation. This controversy seems to have centered around the question of whether the church, as a religious institution, should be actively involved in the anti-slavery movement. The seceding faction, apparently the anti-slavery activists, continued to meet in a loft on Smith Court. In 1843 the secession was complete and in 1848 the secessionists founded the 12th Baptist Church. The remaining congregation launched a revitalization movement and remodelled the African Meeting House in 1855.

Besides serving as a place of worship, the Meeting House was the center of Afro-American civic and educational activities. "The Church, as a physical entity more than earned it sobriquet as the 'Colored People's Faneuil Hall'. Ceremonial and recreational activities of all sorts were held in this the largest and most centrally located structure in the Negro community" (Levesque 1973: 513). William Lloyd Garrison organized the New England Abolitionist Society in the basement school room of the African Meeting House. In the ensuing years many leading Abolitionists including Wendell Phillips and Charles Sumner stood on its platform to denounce the injustices of slavery. It was in this building also, that the first recruiting meeting was held for the organization of the all black Massachusetts 54th regiment during the Civil War.

The church also housed a school for black children for some years. In the late 18th and early 19th centuries the black community chose not to attend Boston public schools and were denied an all black public school. The black parents organized a community school and in 1808 it was moved to the basement of the African Meeting House. In 1834, as a result of a bequest from Abdiel Smith, the Boston school committee financed the building of the Abdiel Smith school next to the African Meeting House to accommodate the growing number of black primary and grammar school students. In the 1840's a new generation of black parents decided to send their children to Boston Public Schools, and were denied entrance. The Smith school was boycotted and black parents protested the expense of sending all Afro-American children in Boston to the school, instead of closer neighborhood schools. In 1855 segregation of schools in Massachusetts was outlawed and the Smith school was closed. This controversy may also have contributed to the factionalism within the African Baptist Congregation.

In the second half of the 19th century the Afro-American population on Beacon Hill grew considerably as a result of migration from the south. Towards the end of the century the population moved to the south end and Roxbury, and the African Meeting House was sold to Congregation Libavitz in 1898.

In the archaeological excavations artifacts and features relating to the appearance of the building and its site were uncovered. When the African Meeting House was built it was surrounded by alleyways on three sides and a court in front. The few houses in the area were wooden structures. The Smith school was built next to the Meeting House in 1834, and in the late 1840's a commercial stable was built behind the Meeting House property extending from Belknap Street to an alley. Other buildings disrupted the flow of traffic through the alleyways. In the 1850's when the church was remodelled the area around the building was more enclosed and took on a new function. Testing the five by fourteen meter area behind the church uncovered three brick piers or footings 2.5 meters from the wall of the stable and spaced at ten foot intervals. These were footings for a two story slate roofed structure show on an 1873 Boston Atlas. This structure had been placed over the original eight foot alleyway and attached to two adjacent buildings. Archaeological testing revealed brick flooring with high coal concentrations indicating that at least one bay was used for coal storage. Conjectured uses for other bays are as a stable or privy.

Part of a drainage system was found (see Figure 2). It has two slate slab covered drains running east west along the alleyway and meeting at a brick lined, wood bottomed terminal box (feature 3). A third drain leaves the terminal and runs north east around the meetinghouse and out toward the street. The brown sandy soil above this drainage system was filled with early to mid-19th

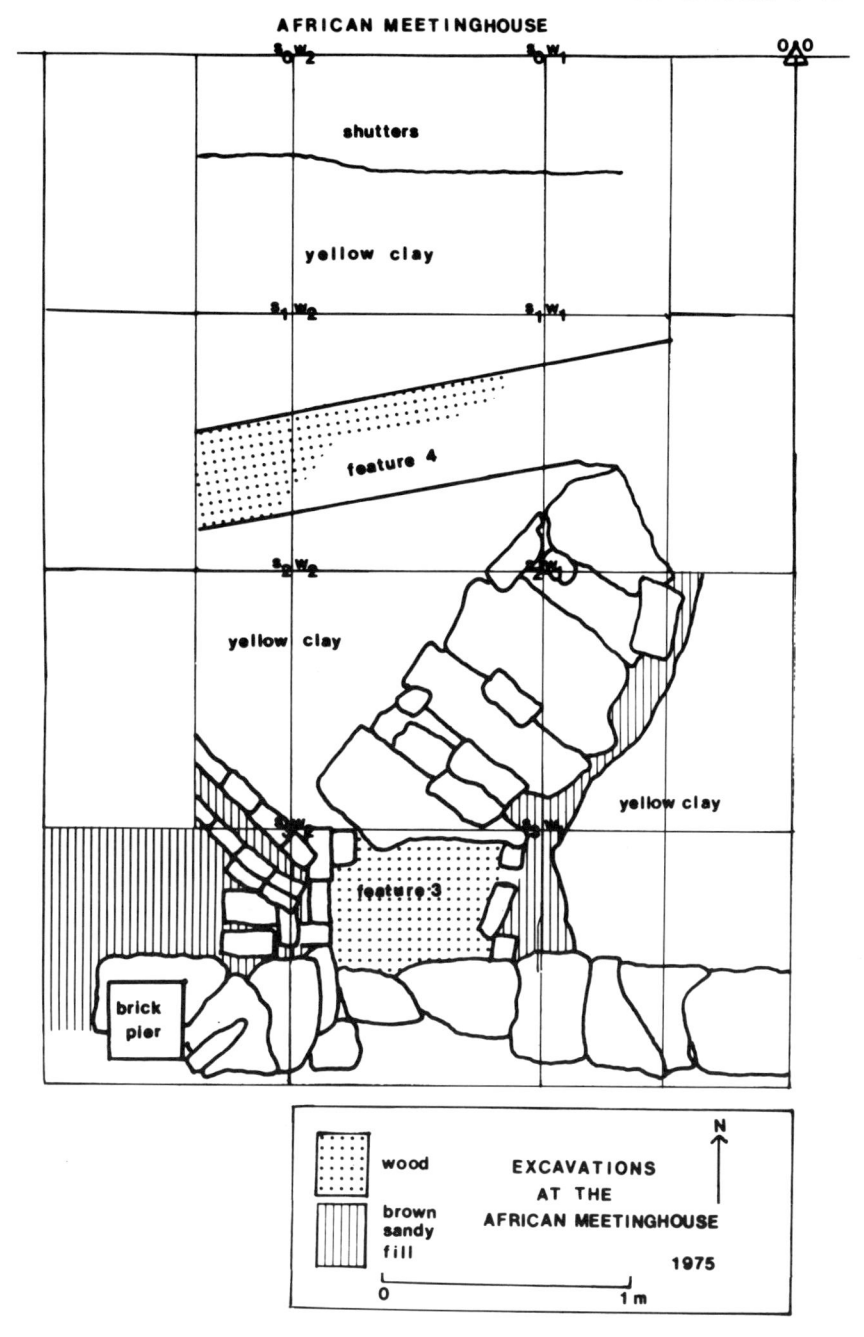

Figure 2. Map of archaeological excavations showing location of drainage system and shutters.

century debris and a great quantity of faunal material. It is our interpretation from preliminary analysis that the drainage system was built and in use in the first half of the 19th century. It was not excavated because it was not fully defined, so its interior appearance and its use have not been investigated. However probably its most important function was to divert water from the church building and carry it down the steep north slope of Beacon Hill. With the discontinued use of the drainage system and the raising of the ground level around the church, a great deal of damage occurred to the walls and basement as a result of water seepage. This process seems to have started in the mid-19th century.

Two finds were made in the excavations which related the post-1850 appearance of the church and the 1890's alterations. Approximately 30 cm. below the surface an early type of gas fixture was found. The architectural historian discovered that it had been located in the gallery rail. It is a twisted bronze or brass candlestick type gaslight which was gilded, had a clear rounded glass lobe with scalloped edges, and it is approximately 22 inches in height. This fixture was probably placed in the church when it was renovated in the 1850's and then replaced later in the century. It was found in a slate and debris level with several late 19th century bottles.

The other architectural evidence found was three pairs of window shutters or interior blinds, which were found set vertically in the ground approximately 32 cm. beneath the surface. The shutters still had the original paints and hardware on them. An 1875 photograph (see Figure 1) of the Meeting House shows similar shutters or blinds on the inside of the second story windows. At first there was no apparent explanation for their presence, but when the shutters were removed, concrete with the imprint of the shutters was found at 49.5 cm. It seems that when the basement was lowered in the 19th century, the foundation walls also had to be extended and the shutters which had been removed from the building were used as forms for the concrete.

Laboratory processing and analysis of the artifacts and faunal material recovered during the excavations at the African Meeting House has been only partially accomplished. Forty of the 164 bags have been fully processed and analyzed. The site was packed with debris, especially in the drainage area. Artifacts which probably related to the school in the basement of the church were found such as slate pencils, pieces of slate to write on, several children's cups, marbles and a china doll's face. Over 4,000 of the 6,119 artifacts catalogued are pieces of pottery, predominantly creamware, pearlware and red earthenware. Many of the pottery fragments can be pieced into identifiable vessels. The refined earthenwares vessels are plates, saucers, mugs and bowls, and the domestic earthenwares are kitchenwares such as butterpots and milk-pans. The refined earthenwares and procelains were manufactured in the late 18th and early 19th centuries and are types which are found on Anglo-American sites of the same period in great quantity. Because the Meeting House was not a residence these artifacts represent objects used and disposed by the community which lived around the church. Further analysis of the artifacts will enable comparisons to be made with collections from other sites of the period in order to identify differing use patterns and form and appearance preferences. The Afro-American community on Beacon Hill was not affluent and this analysis should shed light on the availability of imported ceramics to a different strata of society. In addition 946 bones have been processed, mostly of large mammal, probably cow or pig. Further analysis will provide data on food consumption and butchering techniques in a 19th century urban setting.

Excavation around the African Meeting House will continue in the summers of 1978 and 1979 with support from the National Endowment for the Arts. The drainage system will be fully defined and excavated and testing will be conducted behind the Smith School. Laboratory analysis of the artifacts and faunal material already recovered will be completed, along with further documentary research.

Notes

[1] The building and its congregations have had a variety of names. African Meeting House seems to have been the common term used for the building in the first half of the 19th century and will be used throughout this article. Other designations were the African Baptist Church, the First Independent Baptist Church and the Congregation Libavitz Synagogue.

Bibliography

Detwiller, Frederic C.
    1975   African Meeting House: An Architectural/Historical Analysis. Manuscript on File at the Society for the Preservation of New England Antiquities.

Levesque, George A.
    1975   Inherent Reformers-Inherited Orthodoxy: Black Baptists in Boston, 1800-1873. *Journal of Negro History,* pp. 491-519.

CHAPTER 8
Archaeology of Black American Culture: An Annotated Bibliography

GEOFFREY M. GYRISCO
BERT SALWEN

With the growing interest in Black history and culture has come an increasing awareness of the value of archaeology as a technique for providing information about the past of Black Americans. To aid future researchers in building on widely scattered earlier works, the staff of the Interagency Archaeological Services Division of the Heritage Conservation and Recreation Service, U.S. Department of the Interior, compiled this annotated bibliography. It is extensive but not comprehensive. This edition of the bibliography is a revised and updated version of the one published in 1978 as a supplement to volume 3, number 1 of *11593*, the newsletter of the Office of Archeology and Historic Preservation. Interagency Archaeological Services also plans to publish other material on this subject.

I. Slave Habitations

A. Florida, Kingsley Plantation

Fairbanks, Charles H.
    1972   The Kingsley Slave Cabins in Duval County Florida, 1968. *The Conference on Historic Site Archaeology Papers* 7: 62-93. The Institute of Archeology and Anthropology, University of South Carolina, Columbia.

    A lengthy archaeological report on the excavation of a tabby slave cabin and foreman's cabin.

    1968   Florida. *Society for Historical Archaeology Newsletter* 1(2): 13.

    Briefly describes the excavation which is reported in detail in the paper listed above.

B. Georgia, Butler Island Plantation

Singleton, Theresa A.
   1979   Slaves and Ex-slave Sites in Coastal Georgia. Paper delivered at the 12th annual meeting, Society for Historical Archaeology, Nashville, Tennessee.

C. Georgia, Cumberland Island, Rayfield

Ascher, Robert and Charles H. Fairbanks
   1971   Excavation of a Slave Cabin: Georgia, U.S.A. *Historical Archaeology* 5: 3-17.

A highly readable and scholarly report on the excavation of a slave cabin. Selection of documents suitable for reading aloud are alternated with descriptions of the archaeological excavation and its findings. It is an attempt to discover and convey a sense of daily life as it may have been experienced by the cabin occupants.

D. Georgia, Saint Simons Island

Fairbanks, Charles H.
   1976   Spaniards, Planters, Ships and Slaves: Historical Archaeology in Florida and Georgia, *Archaeology* 29: 164-172.

Includes a three-page summary of a study of status differences among planter, overseer, and slave, as revealed in the archaeological record at Cannon's Point Plantation (Couper Plantation).

McFarlane, Suzanne S.
   1975   The Ethnohistory of a Slave Community: The Couper Plantation Site. M.A. Thesis, University of Florida, Gainesville.

Mullins, Sue A.
   1979   The Southern Coastal Plantation: View from St. Simon's Island, Georgia. Paper delivered at the 12th annual meeting, Society for Historical Archaeology, Nashville, Tennessee.

Otto, John Solomon
   1975   Status Differences and the Archaeological Record: A Comparison of Planter, Overseer, and Slave Sites from Cannon's Point Plantation (1794-1861, St. Simon's Island, Georgia). Ph.D. Dissertation, University of Florida, Gainesville.
   1977   Artifacts and Status Differences: A Comparison of Ceramics from Planter, Overseer, and Slave Sites on an Antebellum Plantation. *Research Strategies in Historical Archeology*, edited by Stanley South, pp. 91-118. Academic Press, New York.

Through the method of hypothesis testing and quantitative analysis, Otto demonstrates that attributes of ceramics are reliable indicators of social class on an antebellum plantation occupied by an upper-class planter family, middle-class white overseers, and Black slaves. The planter family provided the slaves and overseers with a special class of wares, perhaps judged more durable and suitable for laborers. Differences in ceramic shapes are related to differences in diet.

1979a A New Look at Slave Life. *Natural History* 88 (1): 8-30.

A beautifully illustrated article discussing the quality of slave life based on the archaeological evidence of diet, clothing, housing, medicine, and leisure activities.

1979b Cannon's Point Plantation and the Hardy Banks Farm: Material Living Conditions of Old South Slaves. Paper delivered at the 12th annual meeting, Society for Historical Archaeology, Nashville, Tennessee.

This paper compares Cannon's Point Plantation, where complex status differences between planter, overseer, and slave are highly visible in the archaeological record, with the Hardy Banks Farm of Arkansas, where oral tradition indicates little archaeological evidence of status differences between farmer and slave can be expected.

E. Georgia, near Savannah, Mulberry Grove Plantation

Jackson, Susan
    1976 Current Research: Southeast. *Society for Historical Archaeology Newsletter* 9(3): 15-19.

Includes reference to testing, by Nicholas Honerkamp and Robin Smith, in connection with the preparation of an Environmental Impact Statement which revealed subsurface evidence of the slave quarters.

F. Louisiana, New Iberia, Shadows-on-the-Teche

Shenkel, J. Richard and Jack Hudson
    1971 Historic Archaeology in New Orleans. *The Conference on Historic Site Archaeology Papers* 6: 40-44. The Institute of Archeology and Anthropology, University of South Carolina, Columbia.

Refers to excavations in the slave quarters area of this National Trust property.

G. North Carolina, Latimer House

Jackson, Susan
    1977 Current Research: Southeast. *Society for Historical Archaeology Newsletter* 10(2): 21-24.

Briefly describes the excavations undertaken by Dr. Thomas Loftfield of the University of North Carolina at Wilmington in preparation for the restoration of the slave quarters.

H. South Carolina, near Charleston, Archdale Hall

Jackson, Susan
    1977 Current Research: Southeast. *Society for Historical Archaeology Newsletter* 10(1): 42-45.

Includes reference to work by high school students, under the direction of Kay Scruggs, designed to locate and excavate possible slave cabins endangered by suburban development on the plantation. The Charleston Museum sponsored the project.

I. South Carolina, Berkeley County, Spiers Landing

Drucker, Lesley M.
    1979 Spiers Landing: A Socioeconomic Study of an Undocumented Late Eighteenth Century Site in Berkeley County, South Carolina. Paper delivered at the 12th annual meeting, Society for Historical Archaeology, Nashville, Tennessee.

This paper examines the patterns of relative frequencies of artifacts and food remains in an attempt to determine whether the site is a slave site. The site, dating to about 1800, yielded the posthole and drip line pattern of a small house, and four refuse pits.

J. Tennessee, The Hermitage

Smith, Samuel D.
    1976 An Archaeological and Historical Assessment of the First Hermitage. *Tennessee Division of Archaeology Research Series* 2. Tennessee Department of Conservation, Nashville.

The first Hermitage log cabin complex, established in 1804, was used as slave quarters between about 1830 and 1860.

    1977 Plantation Archaeology at the Hermitage: Some Suggested Patterns. *Tennessee Anthropologist* 2: 152-163.

Summarizes archaeological work at the Hermitage, including excavation of slave quarters, and discusses possible patterns in the use of medicine, ceramics, and beads.

K. Tennessee, Castalian Springs

Smith, Samuel D.
1975 *Archaeological Explorations at the Castalian Springs, Tennessee Historic Site.* Tennessee Historical Commission, Nashville.

A report which includes descriptions of test excavations at two of the slave cabin sites in the slave quarters area of this 19th century farm and resort.

L. Virginia, Kingsmill

Abbitt Outlaw, Merry, Beverley A. Bogley and Alain C. Outlaw
1977 Rich Man, Poor Man: Status Definition in Two 17th-Century Ceramic Assemblages from Kingsmill. Paper delivered at the 10th annual meeting, Society for Historical Archaeology, Ottawa, Ontario.

A quantitative comparison of the ceramics of a household known from documentary evidence to be high on the social and economic scale with the ceramics of a slave household. Greater quantity, the presence of specialized vessels, higher quality wares, and greater storage ability were found to correlate with higher social status.

Kelso, William M.
1976 The Colonial Silent Majority: Tenant, Servant and Slave Settlement Sites at Kingsmill, Virginia. Paper delivered at the 75th annual meeting, American Anthropological Association, Washington, D.C.

M. Virginia, Tutter's Neck

Noel Hume, Ivor
1966 Excavations at Tutter's Neck in James City County, Virginia, 1960-1961. *United States National Museum Bulletin 249; Contributions from the Museum of History and Technology 53,* Washington, D.C.

Briefly describes the excavation of several trash pits associated with slave quarters.

II. Northern Free Black Habitations

A. Houses

1. Delaware, near Wilmington

Ascher, Robert
   1974   How to Build a Time Capsule, *Journal of Popular Culture* 8: 241-253.

Using Weslager's report (1954) of the excavation of a colonial log cabin near Wilmington, Delaware, which was last occupied by a Black man, Ascher turns the list of artifacts into an evocative piece of poetry.

Weslager, C. A.
   1954   The Excavation of a Colonial Log Cabin Near Wilmington, Delaware, *Bulletin of the Archaeological Society of Delaware* 6(1).

2. District of Columbia, Cedar Hill (Frederick Douglass House)

Cotter, John L.
   1977   Current Research: Northeast. *Society for Historical Archaeology Newsletter* 10(4): 7-8.

Includes reference to excavations by John Herron of the National Park Service at the Growlery, a small outbuilding where Douglass spent much time writing and thinking.

Mathews, Fleming W. III
   1976   Prelude to Afro-American Archeology: Excavations at Ceder Hill. M.A. Thesis, Howard University, Washington, D.C.

Reports on archaeological investigations of the well, root cellar, carriage house, stable, and cistern at the Douglass House.

3. Massachusetts, Andover, Black Lucy's Garden

Baker, Vernon G.
   1977   Historical Archaeology at Black Lucy's Garden, Andover, Massachusetts: Ceramics from the Site of a Nineteenth Century Afro-American. *Papers of the Robert S. Peabody Foundation for Archaeology* 8. Phillips Academy, Andover, Massachusetts.

An extensively illustrated report with drawings and photographs of 113 ceramic vessels and a discussion of their significance.

Bullen, A. K. and R. P.
  1945   Black Lucy's Garden. *Bulletin of the Massachusetts Archaeological Society* 6(2): 17-28.

Describes the excavation of a cellar hole, large dump, well, and a possible vegetable cellar at site occupied by a free Black woman in the first half of the 19th century.

4. Massachusetts, Concord

Snow, Cordelia Thomas
  1969   *Excavations at Casey's House.* National Park Service. Minute Man National Park, Massachusetts, Mimeographed, 39 pp.

Describes test excavations at site of a small house in Concord, Massachusetts, thought to have been occupied by a former slave freed after military service in the Revolution. No conclusive evidence was obtained.

B. Communities

1. Massachusetts, Plymouth, Parting Ways

Deetz, James
  1976   Black Settlement at Plymouth. *Archaeology* 29: 207.

One page summary of the excavation results at Parting Ways, a small community located near Plymouth on land granted to four freed slaves after their service in the Continental Army during the American Revolution. Archaeological evidence showed that these men retained much of their African cultural background.

  1977   *In Small Things Forgotten.* Doubleday. New York.

Includes a chapter-length report of the archaeological, documentary, and oral history investigation of this free Black community. Significant finds included high quality but old-fashioned ceramics possibly acquired from the wealthy townspeople of Plymouth, and jars probably made in the West Indies that resemble the shape of West African pottery. The architecture and grouping of the houses reflected the residents' African heritage.

2. New York, Staten Island, Sandy Ground

Schuyler, Robert L.
  1972   Archaeological Dig. *City College Alumnus* 67(5): 12-13. New York.

Schuyler, Robert L.
    1974   Sandy Ground: Archaeological Sampling in a Black Community in Metropolitan New York, *Conference on Historic Site Archaeology Papers* 7: 13-52. The Institute of Archeology and Anthropology, University of South Carolina, Columbia.

Lengthy summary of the archaeological investigations of a Black oystermen's community on Staten Island that has only recently been engulfed by the greater New York metropolitan area. Several house foundations and trash deposits were excavated and a cemetery was studied. The evolution of the community and its economic collapse are discussed.

    1977   Archaeology of the New York Metropolis. *The Bulletin of the New York State Archaeological Association* 69: 1-19.

3. New York, Brooklyn, Weeksville

Anonymous
    1970   Digging It. *Newsweek.* March 30, p. 97.

    1971   Weeksville Now Haven for History. *New York Post* Tuesday, October 5, pp. 2, 7.

Contains a brief summary of the history of this mid-19th century Black community and the interest it has inspired in the mid-20th century.

Gutman, Judith Mara
    1976   Uncovering a Long-Lost Village. *New York Times,* February 22, p. D31.

Briefly describes a show at the Metropolitan Museum of Art on Weeksville and discusses its history and the Weeksville project.

Salwen, Bert and Sarah Bridges
    1974   The Ceramics from the Weeksville Excavations, Brooklyn, New York. *Northeast Historical Archaeology* 3(1): 4-29.

Brief summary of the history of this Black community, its growth and decline during the mid-19th century on what was then the edge of the greater New York metropolitan area. The quantitative analysis of ceramics from the site provided this information. The article also summarizes the community interest in this historical and archaeological project in the late 1960's and the 1970's.

III. Miscellaneous

A. African Meetinghouse, Boston

Bower, Beth Anne
  1977a Historical Archeology Investigations: A Methodology for Developing Insights into Colonial/Early American Life. *Technology and Conservation* 2(3): 32-37.

Briefly mentions the archaeological excavations accompanying the restoration of an 1806 church built for the Black community.

  1977b Archeology Programs at the Museum Of Afro-American History: the African Meeting House and Dig Roxbury. In *New England Historical Archeology: The Dublin Seminar for New England Folklife: Annual Proceedings* 2, edited by Peter Benes, pp. 117-23. Boston University Scholarly Publications, Boston.

Briefly reports on excavations at the African Meeting House. An example of participation in historical archaeology by secondary school students.

B. Afro-Carribean Pottery

Vescelius, Gary S.
  1977 Office of the Territorial Archaeologist. *Information* 2(3): 1-3. Newsletter of the Virgin Islands Bureau of Libraries, Museums and Archaeological Services.

This short article identifies a type of pottery found in the Virgin Islands that was probably made by Black potters, mainly if not exclusively, for use in Black households. It seems to have been fashioned in keeping with an African tradition.

C. Cemeteries

Combes, John D.
  1972 Ethnography, Archaeology and Burial Practices Among Coastal South Carolina Blacks. *Conference on Historic Site Archaeology Papers* 7: 52-61. The Institute of Archeology and Anthropology, University of South Carolina, Columbia.

Describes Black burial practices in the Southeast that are characterized by irregular grave orientation, frequent absence of grave markers, and presence of grave offerings on the surface. The article also discusses associated beliefs and customs.

Cotter, John L.
1977 Current Research: Northeast. *Society for Historical Archaeology Newsletter* 10(2): 12-21.

Includes references to salvage excavation of a Black burial ground at College Landing, near Williamsburg, Virginia, by Carter Hudgins of the Virginia Research Center for Archaeology. Analysis of the muscle attachments suggested that these Blacks were engaged in skilled crafts.

Crosby, Constance and Mathew C. Emerson
1979 Identifying Afro-American Mortuary Customs: An Example from the Parting Ways Settlement, Plymouth, Massachusetts. Paper delivered at the 12th annual meeting, Society for Historical Archaeology, Nashville, Tennessee.

A discussion of the similarities between West African and Afro-American grave decoration practices, supporting an argument that an unusual and controversial fieldstone-paved area and associated artifacts at Parting Ways mark the location of a burial site.

Handler, Jerome S. and Frederick W. Lange
1978 *Plantation Slavery in Barbados: An Archaeological and Historical Investigation.* Harvard University Press, Cambridge, Massachusetts.

A major book-length discussion of New World slavery combining documentary and archaeological evidence. The archaeological evidence was derived primarily from 92 17th-19th century interments in the slave cemetery at Newtown Plantation.

Ferguson, Leland
1979 Review of *Plantation Slavery on Barbados: An Archaeological and Historical Investigation* by Jerome S. Handler and Frederick W. Lange. *American Antiquity* 44(2): 384-385.

Focuses on the lack of visibility of slave village sites. Handler and Lange concentrated on the cemetery when test excavation at the supposed location of the slave habitation area produced little evidence of occupation.

PART TWO
Asian American Culture History

Introduction

There are certain parallels between Afro-American and Asian American culture history in the New World but differences are equally pronounced. Both Africans and Chinese (with which this section is concerned) entered North America through narrow, exploitive economic institutions. Plantation slavery in one case; a newer form of industrial servitude in the other. The Chinese exposure was much shorter and once released from the system they, like Blacks before and after them, gravitated to urban centers.

Archaeology along with documentary history highlight the major difference. Chinese Americans were much more successful at preserving their Old World cultural patterns and resisting acculturation to American society. Whether this perseverance is made possible by a more uniform cultural heritage, differences in the severity of exploitation, or the intrinsic nature of Chinese civilization is not fully understood. Archaeology does show that when the abnormal situations found in railroad and mining camps were replaced by the full community pattern of "Chinatowns," Asian American culture flourished and survived to the present. As a result rich ethnographic and oral historic interpretations are possible with Chinese American archaeological collections that are lacking with other ethnic assemblages.

This is not to say that Chinese American patterns were static or stagnant. Adaptations seen in the remains from the Lower China Store in California counterdict such a view. More generally, change is clearly accelerating in the 20th century. Several factors, including the disruption caused by wars and the breaking of Sino-American ties after 1949, would imply an increasing rate of acculturation for this group and a very different ethnic material manifestation in the future. Yet this weakening of Old World ties may prove temporary. Classical Chinese culture has, of course, been disrupted by the Revolution but a cyclical pattern of contact based on international politics may be emerging. Perhaps Chinese American culture, or some modernizing version of it, may prove to have a much greater longevity than many would now predict.

CHAPTER 9

Food and Fantasy: Material Culture of the Chinese in California and the West, Circa 1850-1900

WILLIAM S. EVANS, JR.

Introduction

The Chinese who were enticed to migrate to California at the time of the Gold Rush in 1849 and after (Bancroft 1890: VII: 336; Bean 1968: 163) and who later provided the bulk of the labor force building the Western Pacific Railroad across the Sierras (1865-1869) (Bancroft 1890: VII: 567), brought with them and sustained a native culture. Some of the material elements of that culture survive in the camps and towns connected with mining, construction, and other work throughout the West.

The surviving material content of Chinese culture in the archaeological context is summarized here. Only those artifacts which are of Chinese origin or manufacture are considered, although archaeological sites often include Euro-American elements as well.

Within the first decade of migration, an active provisioning business appears to have evolved in response to the Chinese presence. A printed checklist—"Prices Current for China Provisions, most suitable in this Market, expressly for Chinese use. San Francisco, 185_"—lists commodities, mostly foodstuffs, but includes paper cigars, tobacco, Chinese caps with gold edges, charcoal, mat bags, and boiled opium.

Sizes and kinds of packaging are also listed. Units may be large—25 and 50 pounds for rice and sugar. Salt pork and dried fish at 100 pounds. Salted duck eggs, 100 to a box; tea in baskets, "Chests of Patna, boiled and fil'ed up in earthen pots, of from 5 to 90 taels a pot." Shrimp sauce, salted radish, salted garlic, salted onions, pickled lemons, oil, and soy are listed specifically by jar.

Boxes and baskets have not survived. Earthenware, stoneware, procelain, and glass objects have. So also metallic and other durable materials.

The dominant elements of the Chinese material culture are the paraphernalia of subsistence—*food*—and those related to relaxation or escape through opium use and to the hope for quick returns through gambling—*fantasy*. There is a residual category of artifacts as well, though of few elements.

Food

Shipping and Storage

Evidence of the shipping and storage of food substances is perserved in the form of a variety of large and small stoneware vessels, most with brown-glazed exteriors. Two large vessels are a recurrent element in the artifact inventory: One, barrel-shaped, wide-mouthed, 40 cm tall, and 32 cm in diameter at the mouth. Associated are pan-like unglazed lids. The other, about the same height, is globose with a constricted mouth and four perforated lugs just below. They may have been bulk soy sauce jars (Maust 1973: 37). A specimen recovered in San Francisco is said to have contained preserved eggs.

Smaller shipping and storage vessels are of four kinds: globose soy sauce bottles with short pour spouts; shouldered, wide-mouthed jars (of two, possibly three, sizes) with saucer shaped baked clay lids in which preserved vegetables may have been imported; and jars with fitted, glazed stoneware lids, possibly of several sizes as well. Other kinds of containers are blue and white glazed jars, often referred to as ginger jars, and a small jar with a bulging angular outline and an unusual mottled iridescent greenish glaze. (See Table 1.)

Food Preparation

The artifacts of food preparation are few. Anderson and Anderson (1977: 365) provide an ethnographic inventory for South Chinese: Wok (basin-shaped, cast iron), metal spoon, wire net spoon, knife or cleaver, small sauce pans, sand pots (coarse-grained earthenware vessels), kettle and pot for tea, mobile clay stoves. Archaeological sites yield pieces of cast iron (wok fragments?) and earthenware pan fragments; metal and wire mesh spoons were recovered at Ventura, California (Benté 1976: 482).

Food Service and Consumption

The ordinary family makes do with a minimum of serving and eating vessels (Anderson and Anderson 1976: 365-366): individual rice bowls, main dish platters, small sauce-and-dip dishes, cups, soup bowls, soup spoons. The archaeological array includes numerous individual bowls as at Donner Summit; fewer soup bowls and serving dishes. Cups and spoons occur mainly in urban sites. So also tea pots and sauce pots (Table 2).

Table 1. Ceramics, – utility wares – sherd/vessel count

	Large, wide-mouthed, barrel-shaped jar	Lid, wide-mouthed, barrel-shaped jar	Globose jar	Large jar fragments, unidentified	Shallow cooking pan	"Wine" bottle	Spouted bottle (soy sauce bottle)	Shouldered jar, wide-mouthed	Unglazed fired-clay lids	Unidentified jar and bottle fragments	Straight sided jar with fitted lid	Fitted lid, straight sided jar	Mottled green-glazed stoneware jar	Lid, green-glazed stoneware jar	Blue and white glazed or slipped "ginger" jar	Totals
Bear Valley, Calif. 1850-	3		12	38		1	2			9						53
Per cent	5.6		29.3	70.4		1.9	3.7			16.7						
Near Columbia, Calif. 1850-	3	2		2		3	5	5		9						41
Per cent	7.3	4.9		4.9		7.3	12.2	12.2		22						
Donner Summit, Calif. 1865-1869	96	83	41	1557	3	2	23	62	31	58	1			1	10	1969
Per cent	4.9	4.2	2.1	79.2	0.2	0.1	1.2	3.2	1.8	3					0.5	
Virginia City, Nev. 1860-1890	70	12	36		13	6	8	50	13	38	1		1			248
Per cent	27.8	4.8	14.3		5.2	2.4	3.2	19.8	5.2	15.1	0.4		0.4			
Harmony Borax Works, Calif. 1883-1888							1266		68							1334
Per cent									5.1							
Riverside, Calif. ca. 1900			1	3	1	10	33	1	2		2		1		2	26
Per cent			3.8	11.5	3.8	38.5	11.5	3.8	7.9		7.7		3.8		7.7	
Ventura,[a] Calif. ca. 1900			1		3	29	22	14	14		3	4	1	1	1	93
Per cent			1.1		3.2	31.2	23.7	15.1	15.1		3.2	4.3	1.1	1.1	1.1	

[a] Figures represent minimum number of vessels.

Table 2. Ceramics — table wares — sherd/vessel count

	Celadon									Four Seasons								Miscellaneous Patterns								
	Double Happiness "rice" bowls	Plants, Three circles and "character," "rice" bowls	"Rice" bowls	Sauce dishes	"Tea" cups	Small cups	"Wine" cups	Spoons	"Rice" bowls	Serving ("noodle") bowl	Large serving dishes	"Tea" cups	Sauce dishes (small)	Sauce dishes (very small)	"Tea" cup	Small cups	Spoons	Not identifiable	"Rice" bowls	"Tea" cups	Small cups	Sauce dishes	Spoons	Cylindrical tea pot	Spouted pots, other	Unique, unusual, unidentified	Totals
Bear Valley, Calif. 1850-	3	23			14	1				6														1	3		51
Per cent	5.9	45.1			27.5	2				11.8														2	5.9		
Nr. Columbia, Calif. 1850-		3			1					1																1	6
Per cent		50			16.7					16.7																16.7	
Donner Summit, Cal. 1865-69[a]	827	104	3		33	6		6	7	12	30		1	6	1	2	8	22	1						9		1019
Per cent	81.2	10.2	0.3		3.2	0.6		1.2	1.4	1.2	6		0.1	1.2	0.2	0.2	1.6	2.2	0.2						0.9		
Virginia City, Nev. 1860-90	40	73	74	1	49	4			2	64	30		30			4		88						5	5	7	503
Per cent	8	14.5	14.7	0.2	9.7	0.8			1.6	12.7	6		6			0.8		17.5						1	1	1.4	
Harmony Borax Works 1883-88		82	9																				1				92
Per cent		89.1	9.8																				1.1				
Riverside, Cal. ca. 1900		4	3		3	1		2	2	5	2		2	5		2	4		11	10	1		4	6		4	51
Per cent		7.8	5.9		5.9	2		1.6	1.6	9.8	3.9		3.9	4.1		3.9	7.8			19.6	2		7.8	11.8		7.8	
Ventura, Cal.[a] ca. 1900		17	11		5	2				16	3		4			4	6		11	11	3	2	8	1	2	7	122
Per cent		13.9	9		4.1	1.6				13.1	2.5		3.3			3.3	4.9		9	9	2.5	1.6	6.6	0.8	1.6	5.7	

[a] Figures represent actual vessel count.

92

Table 3. Miscellaneous artifacts, fragments of artifacts

	Opium Pipes	Opium Cans, Tops, Bottoms, Sides	Opium Cans, Metal Strips	Opium Lamp Covers	Glass Gaming Pieces, Black	Glass Gaming Pieces, White	Coins, Chinese	Coins, Annamese	Discs, Metal	Dominos, Chinese	Medicine Bottles	Ink Stone
Bear Valley, Calif. 1850-												
Near Columbia, Calif. 1850-	1											
Donner Summit, Calif. 1865-1869	154	66	49		4	2	15		5		1	1
Virginia City, Nev. 1860-1890	3	6	3				5				4	
Harmony Borax Works, Calif. 1883-1888		1	1		2	5	2			6		
Riverside, Calif. ca. 1900							72	3			7	
Ventura, Calif. ca. 1900	21	Not counted		5	16	95					28	

Fantasy

Opium Smoking Paraphernalia

The archaeological inventory includes ceramic pipe bowls, metal pipe ferrules, and the tops, bottoms, sides, and soldering strips of brass 5-tael (6-2/3 oz.) opium cans of complex construction.

Gambling

Gaming pieces include brass "cash" and lenticular glass "buttons," black and white. The latter have been attributed to the game *wei chi* (Japanese, *go*) (Benté 1976: 478; Kleeb 1976: 504), but more probably have to do with *fan tan* (cf. Culin 1891, 1896; cf. also Goss 1958: 78-79). Counterfeit coins and Annamese coins are reported from Ventura, California (Kleeb 1976: 503). According to Culin (1891: 6), "The brass cash are not used as counters upon the board, leaden pieces from Annam, nai ts'in, 'dirt cash,' being substituted to prevent confusion." At Donner Summit, California, thin discs of metal the size of Chinese coins were recovered and may have had a comparable role. (See Table 3 for distributions.)

Residuum

The remainder of the inventory of artifacts recovered from Chinese occupation sites include medicine bottles (often referred to as opium bottles) of clear, colorless glass, rectangular in cross-section and with short tubular necks. Other sizes and shapes are known (Chu and Chu 1973: 135; Figure 167). A fragment of a black stone ink stone was recovered at Donner Summit. A brown-glazed stoneware stand fragment with a short leg (unglazed) and a depression on the upper, glazed surface to accommodate the legs of another vessel comes from Riverside, California (cf. photograph in Maust 1973: 79). Maust speaks of a ceremonial urn and stand.

Conclusion

The inventory of artifacts of Chinese origin does not stand out for its diversity. I have placed the artifacts in two nearly exclusive categories having to do with food, indeed an important dimension of south Chinese culture (Anderson and Anderson, 1977), and with escape from reality or relaxation or entertainment, the Chinese fantasy world. Only a few artifacts fail to fall into one or the other of these two categories.

How do we account for these characteristics of the archaeological culture. First, Chinese material culture is a wood, bamboo, and paper culture. Second, the Chinese may have taken good care of their material possessions (see Anderson and Anderson for a statement of attitudes and values; cf. also Franck, 1925: 115 on the repair of broken ceramics). It is notable, for example, that no brass tobacco pipe bowls have been found. Third, Chinese society in the West was mainly a single-sex society, above all in the construction and labor camps (see Goss 1958: 77-78 for observations on the occasional appearance of Chinese women at the Great Western Quicksilver Mine during the last quarter of the 19th century). It is also notable, perhaps, that in certain spheres of activity, behavior was highly individualized. At the Great Western, for example, each individual lived in his own shack and prepared his own meals (Goss 1958: 66; but cf. also Anderson and Anderson 1977: 366 and Chinn 1969: 44). This may serve to explain the differences in artifact content when comparing a railroad construction site like Donner Summit with a townsite like Virginia City where a greater variety of ceramic forms makes its appearance (see Tables 1–3), in response, perhaps, to a more settled and possibly increasingly complex social system, the appearance of women in greater numbers, and the establishment of families.

Acknowledgments

Gratitude is expressed to the staff of the California Historical Society and its Library for providing access to and a copy of the checklist of "Prices Current for China Provisions, ..." and to the staff of Department of Special Collections, University Research Library, University of California, Los Angeles, for a copy of Culin's *The Gambling Games of the Chinese in America* (1891).

Bibliography

Anderson, E. N., Jr., and Marja L. Anderson
    1977 *Modern China: South.* In Food in Chinese Culture: Anthropological and Historical Perspectives. K. C. Chang, ed. pp. 317-382. New Haven and London: Yale University Press.

Bean, Walton
    1968 *California: An Interpretive History.* Second Edition, 1973. New York: McGraw-Hill Book Company.

Benté, Vance G.
    1976 *"Good Luck, Long Life."* In The Changing Faces of Main Street: A Report prepared for the Redevelopment Agency, City of San Buenaventura ... Roberta S. Greenwood, ed. pp. 457-495. San Buenaventura: Redevelopment Agency of the City of San Buenaventura.

Chinn, Thomas W., ed.
  1969 *A History of the Chinese in California: A Syllabus.* San Francisco: Chinese Historical Society of America.
Culin, Stewart
  1891 *The Gambling Games of the Chinese in America.* In Publications of the University of Pennsylvania, Series in Philology, Literature and Archaeology I: 4: 1-17. Philadelphia: University of Pennsylvania Press.
  1896 *The Origin of Fán T'án.* Overland Monthly 28: 153-155.
Franck, Harry A.
  1925 *Roving Through Southern China.* New York and London: The Century Co.
Goss, Helen Rocca
  1958 *The Life and Death of a Quicksilver Mine.* Los Angeles: Historical Society of Southern California.
Kleeb, Gerald N.
  1976 *Analysis of the Coins from a Chinese Trash Pit in Ventura.* In The Changing Faces of Main Street: A Report prepared for the Redevelopment Agency, City of San Buenaventura . . . Roberta S. Greenwood, ed. pp. 497-508. San Buenaventura: Redevelopment Agency of the City of San Buenaventura.
Maust, Don A. ed.
  1973 *Collectable Chinese Art and Antiques.* Uniontown, Penna.: E. G. Warman Publishing, Inc.
Teague, George A. and Lynette O. Shenk
  1977 *Excavations at Harmony Borax Works: Historical Archeology at Death Valley National Monument.* Western Archeological Center Publications in Anthropology No. 6. U.S. Department of the Interior, National Park Service.

CHAPTER 10

The West Coast Chinese and Opium Smoking

PATRICIA A. ETTER

Lured by the prospect of attaining instant wealth, thousands of Chinese came to the California gold fields in the mid-1850's, hoping later to return home, rich and respected. More and more immigrants came, then dispersed. By 1882, approximately 132,000 Chinese (Chinn 1969) were living and working in the western United States. A great many found employment in railroad construction and lived in temporary campsites along the lines. Others settled in hastily constructed Chinatowns and camps near mines, canneries or agricultural fields.

One of the culture elements introduced by these immigrants was the practice of opium smoking, and physical remains of this custom—opium pipe bowls—are usually found in areas of former Chinese occupation. These bowls, in their fragmentary state, might not be recognized by the historical archaeologist. The object of this report, therefore, is to describe these unusual artifacts, their use, and to suggest a number of categories for cataloguing different types of bowls. The opium pipe bowls that served as a basis for this paper were obtained from surface collections at several railroad campsites near Donner Summit, California (occupied from 1866 to 1867), and from a four-block area that was formerly Chinatown in Virginia City, Nevada, and was occupied between 1865 and 1875.

The opium pipe bowl is an integral part of the opium pipe. Made of earthenware or stoneware, it is a detachable unit, hollow, and basically bell-shaped. In Figure 1, I have named the various pipe-bowl parts. As the diagram shows, the bowl is completely enclosed at the bell end. This covering is slightly convex and is the top of the bowl. It is called the *Smoking Surface*. A center hole, the *Aperture*, is large enough to admit a darning needle. The *Neck* supports a *Connecting Flange*, and this part fits into the opium pipe. Bowls are either faceted or plain. The bowl in Figure 1 features a flaring rim, while the bowl in Figure 3 is straight-sided. The term *Shoulder* is used to describe the cup

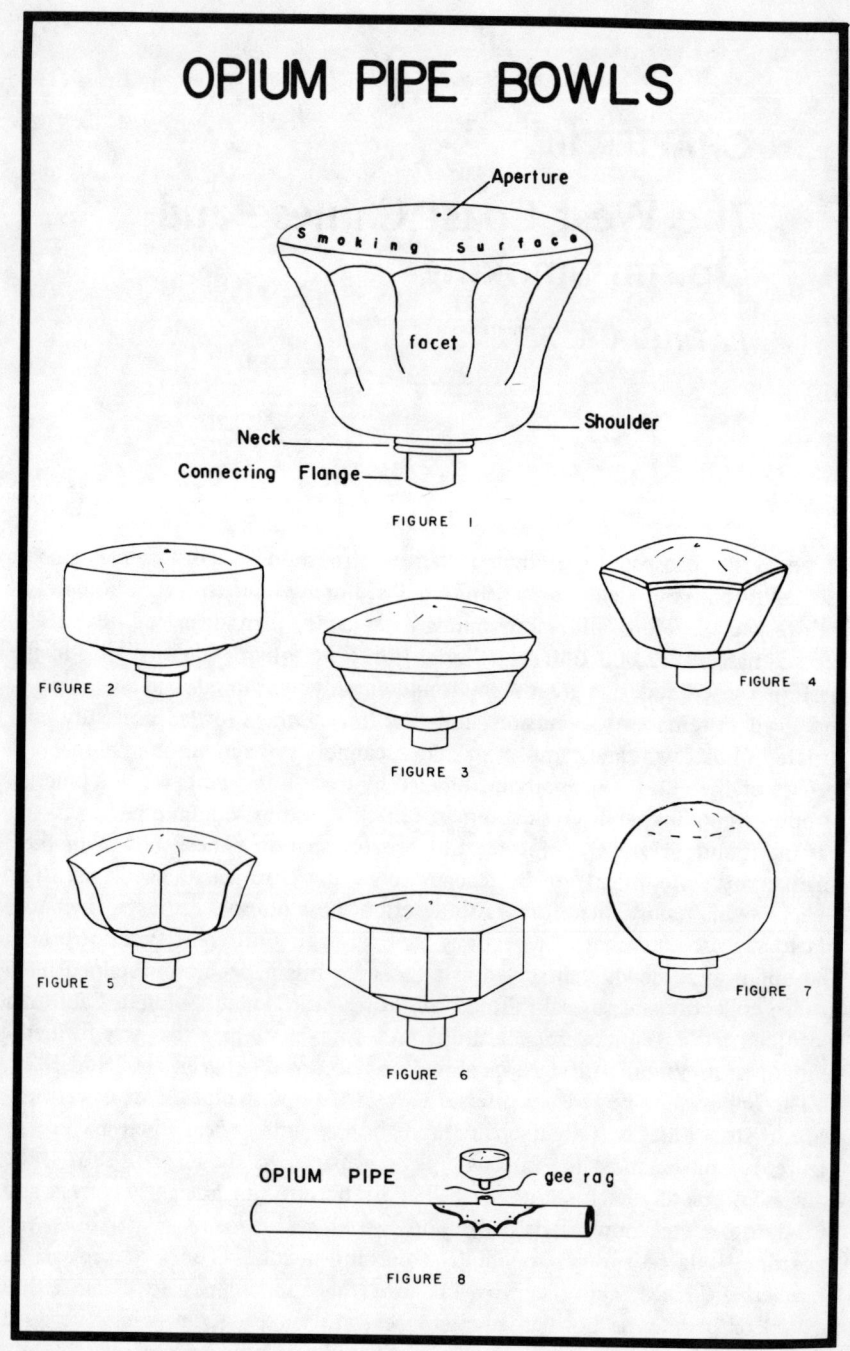

OPIUM PIPE BOWLS

FIGURE 1 — Aperture, Smoking Surface, facet, Neck, Shoulder, Connecting Flange

FIGURE 2

FIGURE 3

FIGURE 4

FIGURE 5

FIGURE 6

FIGURE 7

FIGURE 8 — OPIUM PIPE, gee rag

P.A. Etter

portion, and these shoulders are either square or round. Most pipe bowls measure from 4 to 5 cm high (including the neck and connecting flange), and smoking surfaces range from 5 to 7.8 cm in diameter. Harney and Cross (1975: 57) learned that there was good reason for the design of the bowl for "... the dimensions and materials ... were very carefully calculated to produce a maximum amount of *distillation* and a minimum amount of *incineration* of the opium in the process of smoking."

Figure 8 shows how an opium bowl fits into a brass or copper fitting positioned on the opium pipe. This fitting is from six to eight inches from the mouthpiece. The pipe, usually made of bamboo, was approximately two feet in length with a diameter of two inches. Opium pipes are not likely to be found in archaeological sites although fittings are occasionally recovered. The gee rag is a piece of cloth which helped to secure the bowl to the pipe and which also collected the ashes from smoking. These ashes were often mixed with water and drunk; the resulting concoction was known as Yen Shee Shue.

In addition to an enclosed space or opium den, the opium smoker required a certain amount of equipment for his indulgence. According to the San Francisco Chronicle of February, 1886, this was called a *Layout* and could be purchased for as little as six dollars. The pipe was called *Yen Teung* while the opium bowl was known as *Yin Low*. The needle was termed *Yen Hauk* and a curved tool, *Yen Shee Gow*, was used to scrape the residual ash from the inside of the pipe bowl. A lamp, *Yin Tene,* was fueled with vegetable or nut oil; it supplied a constant flame during smoking.

Smoking opium was a viscous liquid—like molasses—and had to be cooked before smoking. A pea-sized portion of opium was impaled on the needle and heated over the cooking lamp until it became soft, like gum, as its moisture evaporated. The smoker then placed the opium-laden needle into the aperture of the pipe bowl and withdrew the needle. The opium remained on the top of the bowl, around the aperture like a small doughnut. Ideally, the smoker reclined on a couch, and holding the pipe at an angle to the flame of the lamp, inhaled and sucked the flame against the opium. The opium burned to smoke, and the smoker breathed this in, much cooled down through the pipe. His smoke was finished in about thirty seconds.

The pipe bowls were made in at least two sections by pressing clay into a mold and many bowls still bear the fingerprints of their creators. The smoking surface was molded separately and slip-welded to the bowl. In some cases, it appears that a brush was inserted through the neck to further seal the bowl and smoking surface at the inside rim.

The artisans employed many grades of clay to make pipe bowls. We have recovered stoneware bowls at the two sites, but most bowls were orange earthenware, either burnished to a finish or covered with a clear glaze. However, some of the stonewares and other bowls of miscellaneous clay types were slip-covered with orange, grey or brown pigments. Many bowls carry potter's marks or geometric designs along the rim or shoulder; these were block-stamped. Some bowls appear with raised or incised bands encircling the body. It must be pointed out that opium pipe bowls fracture easily and the researcher may recover small fragments. Too, some bowls fracture only at the rim and along one side as if they had fallen from the pipe.

I have categorized the bowls by rim and bowl shape. They are:

Figure 1 *Circular Smoking Surface – Flaring Rim, faceted:* These bowls are thinly constructed from orange earthenware and fragment easily.

Figure 2 *Circular Smoking Surface – Straight-sided, plain:* Bowls of this type were made from many clays, especially stoneware and earthenware. They can appear with or without incised or raised decorative bands.

Figure 3 *Circular Smoking Surface – Flaring Rim, plain:* A bowl of this type often has decorative bands and is made of earthenware or stoneware.

Figure 4 *Hexagonal Smoking Surface – Flaring Rim, faceted:* This bowl is made of coarse-tempered clay.

Figure 5 *Octagonal Smoking Surface – Flaring Rim, faceted:* Made of stoneware, bowls of this type have a highly polished smoking surface.

Figure 6 *Octagonal Smoking Surface – Straight-sided, faceted:* These bowls were usually made of orange or black earthenware. Stamped geometric designs often appear along the rim and/or shoulder.

Figure 7 *Round Bowl:* Many round bowls in private collections or museums are procelain but those from work sites in the west are earthenware. The shape varies from round to oval.

This completes the categories into which the opium pipe bowls were fitted. I have compared the bowls with other collections, photographs or illustrations to test the classifications. They too, show many of the variations discussed above and can be fitted into the different categories. It appears, therefore, that the bowl shapes were standardized to optimize the distillation process in opium smoking. Variety was achieved with different clays, design elements, colors, and smoking surface shapes.

At the same time, some bowl shapes seems to call for a particular type of clay. For example, Figure 1 illustrates a bowl that is typically of orange earthenware. The bowl in Figure 5 appears in stoneware. More study may reveal that certain shapes were fashioned with a specific clay.

The Donner Summit construction workers smoked mainly from the plain, burnished orange earthenware bowls. On the other hand, the residents of Virginia City Chinatown showed more individuality in their choice of pipe bowls and smoked from more slip-covered clay and stoneware bowls. Again, by comparison with collections from other areas of California, it is more likely that the cheaper, thinly-constructed earthenware bowls will be recovered at work sites. A higher percentage of varietal, better constructed stonewares and clay bowls will probably be found in Chinatowns and areas of more permanent occupation.

Bibliography

Chin, Thomas W., Editor, H. Mark Lai, Philip P. Choy, Associate Editors
    1969   *A History of the Chinese in California.* San Francisco: Chinese Historical Society of America.

DeQuille, Dan (William Wright)
    1947   *The Big Bonanza.* New York: Alfred A. Knopf.

Harney, Malachi L. and John C. Cross
    1975   *The Narcotic Officer's Notebook.* Springfield: Charles C. Thomas.

San Francisco Chronicle
    1886   *The Opium Habit: Alarming Increase of the Vice.* Monday, February 1.

CHAPTER 11

The Archaeology of 19th Century Chinese Subsistence at the Lower China Store, Madera County, California

PAUL E. LANGENWALTER II

Introduction

The California Gold Rush resulted in a multinational influx of wealth seekers. The Chinese, among others, were drawn to the Sierran mines by tens of thousands. Their migration resulted in the population of numerous camps and towns throughout the mining districts which form an integral part of California's history. Late in Sierran gold mining history a handful of Chinese operations persisted long after the Gold Rush was over. Among these was a colony of several hundred Chinese along the Fresno River. Gold mining in this portion of the Southern Mining District began in earnest in the 1860's after the failure of the Fresno Indian Farm and remained a local concern into the 20th century although organized Chinese efforts deteriorated in "the 1880's."

Two stores were established in Hidden Valley along the Fresno River to supply the Chinese miners. Both were ultimately under the ownership of Ah Sun, a Chinese merchant. Ah Sun's initial establishment and presumed residence was the Lower China Store which operated from "the 1860's" to 1885. Both of these stores served the entire community including the Chinese, local Indians who had previously depended on the trading posts of J. D. Savage, L. Leach and the Fresno Indian Farm agents (Elliot 1882: 176), and the more recent Anglo settlers (Scheidt 1966: 36-37).

The Lower China Store was excavated during the Hidden Reservoir Archaeological Project under the direction of Franklin Fenenga. The project was jointly undertaken by California State University, Long Beach, the National Park Service and U.S. Army Corps of Engineers, Sacramento. The site was excavated by field crews under the direction of Claudia Nissley and John Murray.

The Lower China Store was originally a one room adobe structure with later wood frame additions including at least two additional rooms and a blacksmith shop. A trash pit located immediately north of the structure was excavated concurrently, producing the bulk of the sample. It was found to represent a homogeneous short-term deposition dating from circa. 1883-1885. The refuse recovered reflects two aspects of Chinese subsistence: debris from the operation of the store and debris from the resident's activities.

The data gained from the excavation of the Lower China Store provides insight into local Chinese subsistence and the economic network to which it belonged. This paper is principally concerned with plant and faunal remains as primary evidence of subsistence. The inclusion of metal, ceramic and glass containers has been necessary to complete the analysis of the subsistence pattern although these are secondary lines of evidence which rarely do more than infer the presence of certain foodstuffs.

Chinese Subsistence

During the Gold Rush, prejudice against Chinese success quickly led to local and state laws which discriminated against foreign miners (Heizer and Almquist 1971: 151-177). This forced many Chinese miners to seek work elsewhere and led to the early development of fishing and farming industries along the California coast. Some Chinese established local shops and import-export buinesses. Many of these were located in San Francisco, Sacramento and Stockton to supply stores in the Sierran Nevada and the Great Valley. This entry into California business provided the basis for the greater economic network which supplied the numerous stores serving the Chinese.

The primary reason that local stores were able to exist was due to the wish of Chinese to maintain their traditional lifestyle. Spier's (1958a) synthesis of historic records dealing with Chinese subsistence suggests that considerable effort was expended in the maintenance of a traditional diet. The Chinese propensity to maintain their culture is mentioned by several authors (Nordhoff 1874; Spier 1958a and 1958b) who discuss culinary habits. The breadth of maintenance can be seen in the U.S. Customs House records described by Spier (1958a: 80) which lists forty-six imported items, dominantly dried fruits, vegetables, meats and eggs.

Wherever groups of Chinese worked they normally had both a store with traditional provisions and a Chinese cook included in the contractual arrangements. In such situations foods were prepared in a traditional manner and served with rice and tea. In one store serving a Merced Railroad gang in 1870, the inventory included dried oysters, dried cuttlefish, dried fish, rice crackers, dried bamboo sprouts, salted cabbage, Chinese sugar, dried seaweed, Chinese bacon, dried abalone, various dried fruits and vegetables (Nordhoff 1874: 190).

Additionally, the stores provided "... pipes, bowls, chopsticks ... cast-iron bowls ..., lamps, joss paper, Chinese writing paper, pencils and india ink." Local stores were major factors in cultural maintenance and were probably accessible to most Chinese where their numbers were sufficient to support such an establishment.

The sum of Spier's synthesis and the conclusions drawn by other authors agree that the traditional subsistence pattern varied spatially and temporally, or to the nature of acculturation derived as a function of intercultural contact and isolation. An example of pattern variation can be seen in the Chinese meat source. It has been documented that dried and preserved meats were available through import and that canned fish were produced along the coast but a fresh supply would be a matter of local availability. Elliot's (1882: 87) description of an Anglo hog farm based on a Chinese clientele provides evidence of a locally derived protein source predicated on intercultural contact, an indication that certain aspects of the subsistence network were not provided for in the Chinese economic strategy and remained under local control in spite of transoceanic trade or the coastal fishing and farm industries.

The historic information available suggests that Chinese subsistence is composed of an emphasis on plant foods supplemented by animal foods, primarily seafood and fowl with lesser amounts of pork. The modern Chinese market in California reflects this generalized pattern with some modification through the introduction of Anglo foods.

Using this model, the occurrence of a Chinese store along the Fresno River suggests the maintenance of a traditional subsistence pattern by the Chinese miners. Following Spier's synthesis (1958a), it may be hypothesized that the subsistence pattern would have undergone minimal acculturation and that both "... foods, culinary wares, the implements of production and the techniques of processing ..." were maintained. Since the historic record indicates that some introductions to Chinese subsistence occurred in spite of efforts toward maintenance, a companion hypothesis follows: These acquired non-Chinese culture traits may have been locally derived and a result of the functions of intercultural contact and isolation. The magnitude of these culture traits would be the sum of scarcity of traditional foodstuffs and the intensity and duration of intercultural exposure.

Artifactual Evidence

The biologic sample used in this study is composed of 1063 specimens representing twelve taxa. These were identified following the principles described by Simpson (1945) in conformance with accepted taxonomic procedure.

Among the taxa represented, several species are not associated with cultural activity. The land snail (*Helminthaglypta* sp.), California ground squirrel (*Citellus beecheyi*) and southern pocket gopher (*Thomomys bottae*) appear at the site as a result of their natural activities (cf. Langenwalter 1976).

Several other species may or may not have had economic value. The freshwater mussel (*Margaritifera margaritifera*) and the western pond turtle (*Clemmys marmorota*) could have been brought to the store for use as curiosities or occurred as residual remains from an earlier aboriginal occupation. The domestic cat (*Felis catus*) remains may have been from a pet or an animal used as food. A fossil horse (*Equus* sp.) tooth from the sample apparently represents the use of dragon bone medicinal preparations although the specimen is of local origin rather than imported.

The species utilized for food at the Lower China Store include a walnut (*Juglans* sp.), cuttlefish (*Sepia* sp.), the Sacramento perch (*Archoplites interruptus*), chicken (*Gallas gallus*), pig (*Sus scrofa*), sheep (*Ovis aries*) and cow (*Bos taurus*). The single walnut shell recovered from the site was presumably imported but whether it is the European or Oriental variety is not determinable. Dried cuttlefish is a common seafood found in modern Chinese markets. It occurs with and without the cuttlebone (the portion found at the site) and is an imported item. The perch represented by one specimen is an indigenous species. Its presence indicates the use of the Fresno River as a source of fresh fish.

Chickens are represented in the sample by two specimens which are insufficient to determine specific anatomical attributes or to propose breed affinities. The absence of egg shell also suggests the nominal use of this animal by the proprietor.

Pigs are the most common species in the sample, being represented by more than 1000 specimens from fifteen individuals. Using tooth eruption dates and wear patterns, the specimens fall into three age categories: 8 to 20 months, greater than 8 to 20 months and an older adult. The similarity of the eruption and wear stages in the first two categories indicates a slaughter age of 19 ± 2 months. This coincides with the end of rapid growth in swine after which it becomes more costly to produce animals of greater weight. Thus, a least cost principle is evident in the slaughter of pigs.

Sheep are sparsely represented in the sample by a metacarpal and illium fragment. The illium has been cut by a hand saw. The use of this tool is an Anglo culture trait that has no apparent parallel in Chinese butchering technology, indicating that lamb was obtained from the Anglo community.

The occurrence of a vertebra and two scapula fragments of the cow indicates that beef was a supplementary source of meat. The scapulae were cut with a hand-held saw to produce shoulder clod roasts. Specimens identical to these have been recovered from the 19th century Anglo assemblages of several coastal southern California sites. The occurrence of these specimens indicates exchange with the Anglo community.

Two types of metal food containers found at the site were the sardine tin and the hole-in-top can. Twenty-one sardine tins of six and nine ounce sizes were recovered. The frequency of these infer the use of sardines (*Sardinops caeruleus*) as a regular food source. The origin of these packed fish is almost certainly the California coast around San Francisco which had a well developed fishing industry for over a decade. Twenty-three hole-in-top cans of sixteen and twenty-four ounce sizes were recovered which had been cut open to remove the contents which may have been either fruit, vegetables or meat. Also occurring were a capped container for "Golden Gate Baking Powder" and several five gallon rectangular cans which may have contained bulk foods.

The ceramic containers are all of Chinese origin. They are standard brown ware constructed from a light colored paste and coated by a vitreous brown glaze. These containers are discussed in detail by Chace (1976). Three types were recovered from the Lower China Store. The first is the remains of three large barrel jars of 40 to 50 centimeters in height. These were covered with an unglazed lid and filled with various foodstuffs. Modern informants have stated that they were used for shipping preserved eggs in the recent past. A second type is a soy sauce bottle (Chace 1976: 517; Figure 1b) represented by three fragmentary vessels. These bottles have a capacity of about 40 ounces and contained soy sauce. The last type is a shouldered food jar (Chace 1976: 517-519; Figure 2b) represented by two fragmentary vessels. These were produced to hold one or more pounds of preserved vegetables, bean curd and perhaps other items (Chace 1976: 119).

Table wares included ceramic rice bowls with the Three Circles and Dragonfly pattern (Chace 1976: 523), a small blue on white bowl and Celadon tea cups, all of which are Chinese export wares. The only Anglo ceramic is a white ironstone platter.

Glass beverage containers occurred in numerous varieties. These were principally beer, wine and French Square forms. Following the data provided by Switzer (1974) and the marks on some of the bottles, the beverages consumed at the site included beer, wine, champagne, whiskey, bitters, schnapps and possibly soda pop. Products definitely identified include "Budweiser Lager Beer," "Dr. J. Hostetter's Stomach Bitters" and "Udolpho Wolfe's Schiedan Schnapps."

Discussion

The sample provides evidence of Chinese subsistence activity in three areas: butchering techniques, general subsistence and the economic network in which the Chinese store operated.

The techniques used in butchering are obvious on the pig, sheep and cow remains. The pig remains are the only specimens which may be identified as having been butchered by Chinese while the sheep and cow remains are from finished cuts of meat traded to the store from local Anglos, having been cut using Anglo tools and technique. Alternately, the pigs were butchered exclusively with a cleaver and the possible assistance of a knife. The diagnostic attributes of the cut marks on the pig bone indicate the use of a Chinese cleaver as opposed to its European counterpart.

The Chinese cleaver is a narrow bladed, straight backed tool sharpened high on its side with a bevel similar to a razor. The cutting motion of this tool results in a narrow cut and normally clean separation of bone which is distinguishable from the cut of a European cleaver. The latter has a wider blade with a distinct bevel extending five to ten millimeters up its side. It produces a wider V shaped cut often subtended by an impacted fracture at the point of contact. Occasionally an irregular edge on the Chinese tool will leave several parallel micro ridges following the direction of the cut embedded on dense bone specimens. The European tool with its broader blade cannot leave similar markings.

The Chinese tool is used in much the same way as the European tool, with the blade used for cleaving and the back as a hammer. The hammering motion serves to separate incompletely cleaved bones or to fracture limb bones for the marrow or soup bones. The Chinese cleaver appears to be used more often as a cutting blade (knife) than the European form, in that the Chinese butcher wastes bear more blade cuts than do specimens from the 19th century Spanish/Mexican and Anglo components from the Avila Adobe or Machado-Silvas House. My observations of modern Chinese and Anglo butchers indicate that the cleaver is often, but not always used, as a cutting device by the former, while the latter regularly switches to a knife.

Further examination of the faunal remains have revealed the following patterns. The butchered pork remains indicate that much of the carcass had the meat stripped from it and the limb bones shattered for marrow or use as soup bones. The head was severed immediately behind the skull and split down the midline for brain extraction while the mandibles were broken and cut away to remove the tongue. The few remaining portions of the axial skeleton, other than the skull, suggest that the carcass was halved during butchering. Meat cuts similar to a rib chop and short ribs were taken from the back and sides.

Observations concerning the appendicular skeletal parts show that the forelimb was halved at the elbow. Meat cuts respresented in the sample include pigs knuckles and pigs feet. The hindlimb was detached from the carcass by cutting through the pelvis. Cuts of meat from the hindlimb include hocks, feet and possibly butt roasts.

The sample was composed largely of butchering waste, including skull and dentary fragments, bone splinters and fragments of limb bone shafts. Most of the original skeletal bone was sold with the meat and left the store premises. Some of this bone, called tablewaste which would be discarded during cooking or after dining, does occur in the sample. It includes most of the vertebra, rib, distal limb bone, manus and pes elements. These were used to determine the few cuts of meat described above. This type of boney waste differs from butcher waste in that the cutting of these bones would not have been accomplished unless they were to be included in specific cuts. Butcher waste is the remnant of these cutting operations which is removed previous to sale.

The evidence of butchering is cross culturally significant. Since marks resulting from the Chinese type cleaver can be distinguished from those of the European cleaver, the ethnicity of butchering can be established. This allows the differentiation of Chinese butchered samples and Spanish or Mexican butchered samples although both have been butchered with a cleaver. The separation of Anglo butchered samples can be based on the presence of hand sawed specimens since the Chinese and the Spanish or Mexicans did not use this instrument for butchering until recently. The exclusive use of the Chinese or Oriental type cleaver probably assisted by a knife also indicates that this method of food preparation had not become acculturated.

The archaeological record of subsistence as represented at the Lower China Store reflects only a small portion of the Chinese subsistence pattern documented by Spier (1958a) from the ethnohistoric records. This is largely the result of the perishability of the plant foods which dominated the Chinese diet. Animal foods are well represented in both contexts and form a basis for comparison. Historic records of vertebrate animal foods explicitly indicate the use of fish, ducks, eggs, chickens and pork as principal food items.

Fish and pork are the primary animal foods consumed at the Lower China Store. While no reliable estimation of the proportions to one another can be determined, the multiplicity of sardine tins and pork bone table wastes indicates that these were commonly consumed. This diet was occassionally augmented with lamb, beef, chicken and perch. The major incongruity of the sample, when compared with the historic record is the paucity of fowl. Only two chicken bones occur, representing one individual, while egg shell and duck bone are completely lacking. This cannot be considered an accident of preservation, but apparently represents the individual preferences of the resident storekeeper. Presumably, eggs and fowl were sold by the store but have left no tangible evidence.

Other foods used by the storekeeper include soy sauce, baking powder and walnuts. The presence of several shouldered food jars indicates that specific traditional foods were used while the numerous tin cans represent dietary replacements or additions. The food items identified from refuse and the imported ceramic food containers, whose contents is not certain, are the types of subsistence refuse expected from a site occupied by a Chinese who adhered to a traditional diet. The principal departure is the occurrence of baking powder which suggests that levined breads had been introduced into the diet.

The presence of numerous liquor bottles in the sample indicates that considerable alcohol was consumed at the store. However, all of the liquor containers are Anglo in origin while no Chinese liquor bottles were recovered. This is in conflict with the apparent conservative nature of the keeper's diet but is in conformance with the function of the store as a source of supply. Presumably, the existing liquor bottles were the discards of the store's patrons and not the keeper.

The ceramic table wares used by the storekeeper are similarly conservative. These are exclusively traditional wares imported from China with the exception of an ironstone platter. The addition of the ironstone is a nominal assimilation into the material culture when compared to the numerous ceramic remains.

Relatively little assimilation of culture traits can be seen in the subsistence and table ware refuse. The assimilations which do occur are strictly single element traits and are insignificant when culture patterns of cognition or behavior are considered. The use of Anglo meat sources and local fish represent simple replacement of food items. If the baking powder represents the introduction of leavened bread baking then the local level of acculturation extends past simple additions to the material culture and encompasses a distinct set of non-Chinese knowledge and behavior patterns which might be considered a significant introduction to the subsistence pattern.

The role of the store as a supplier of meat is not completely understood. The emphasis on pork and its butchering at the store indicates its central role as the principal meat product. This is compatible with traditional Chinese food preferences and is interpreted to reflect local Chinese preferences. Apparently, sheep and beef were not butchered on the premises but obtained from Anglos for the keeper's use. Whether lamb or beef were sold from the store is unknown. Both the infrequent use of these by the keeper and the apparent lack of them for sale indicates a difference in ethnic food preferences in 19th century California which can be observed in the archaeologic record. Lamb and beef each comprise about 6 per cent of the mammalian food refuse, unlike contemporary Spanish/Mexican and Anglo samples in which beef comprises up to 80 per cent of the sample while pork comprises a maximum of 10 per cent.

The economic network to which the store belongs is represented by the types and distribution of subsistence refuse. The food containers serve to provide documentation which would not be tangible if only the primary faunal remains were used. Unfortunately, the use of this secondary resource may be tenuous since there is no proof that they contained food when they reached the site of final deposition.

Using the data at hand, an economic network can be postulated with the store as its focus. Entering the store are imported and local classes of subsistence resources. The imported items are represented by the remains of their containers. These would have been shipped through ports in the San Francisco and Delta regions. The earthenware containers are from China and presumably their contents are of like origin. The metal and glass containers represent foods derived from California and Eastern United States industry. Locally derived resources include pigs, butchered lamb and beef obtained from the Anglo farms, and perch.

The clientele of the store included Anglo farmers and Indians as well as Chinese miners. Chinese ceramics occur in farm sites and aboriginal village sites contemporary with the store operation. The occurrence of Anglo meat cuts at the store suggests that barter was one form of trade engaged in between the Chinese and Anglo residents. The primary purpose of the Chinese stores on the Fresno River was to supply the Chinese miners and laborers. Although their camps have never been located and the trade explicitly defined, the relationship is axiomatic.

Conclusions

A comparison of the ethnohistoric record and a single archaeologic sample from the Lower China Store provide complementary data which reaffirm the ethnohistoric record (Spier 1958a). The archaeological sample is dissimilar to the historic record because of its place in the economic network, accidents of preservation and limitations of the archaeological data drawn from a single sample. However, the congruence of these sets of evidence infers the accuracy of the original assumptions. The archaeological record demonstrates that the Chinese subsistence pattern as it existed during a brief period of gold exploration along the Fresno River was little acculturated. The foods, culinary wares, implements and techniques of production are traditionally Chinese with few exceptions. The manner in which inter-cultural contact and isolation have affected the pattern is in part evident from the archaeological remains. The departures from the traditional pattern are several. The use of a locally bred meat supply and an indigenous freshwater fish represent pragmatism in the replacement or supplementation of existing culture items which are not available. Second is the use of Anglo butchered meat and canned foods representing another replacement of a source of supply. The occurrence of some Anglo table wares does indicate assimilation of the material culture associated with subsistence. While these might be considered acculturation, *sensu lato,* they remain substitutions necessitated by geographic distance. These events do not fit a definition of acculturation on the level of culture patterns (Herskovitz 1964: 169-181) nor do they suggest the cognitive changes necessary to postulate acculturation. Thus, no concrete demonstration of acculturation is evident. This indicates the scarcity of foodstuffs, intensity of intercultural contact, length of exposure or a combination of all were not exerting sufficient pressure to select for the acculturation of the traditional pattern.

The fact that Chinese subsistence does remain intact as seen in both the historical and archaeological investigations suggests several useful implications. Subsistence refuse may be used to identify cultural association based on faunal composition and butchering technique where other means are unavailable, and coupled with historic data it could be used as a temporal indicator. In this sense, subsistence refuse would then fulfill the general functions of other artifact types.

The homogeneity of the Chinese subsistence pattern and its shallow temporal depth may pose interpretive problems in studies of culture change. Some types of change are observable in modern Chinese subsistence patterns such as the abandonment of traditional butchering techniques and the introduction of numerous culture traits in replacement of traditional ones as is visible in cooking apparatus and table wares. This introduction of multiple traits or trait complexes, which modify the structural and cognitive aspects of the subsistence pattern by restructuring behavior patterns, technology, and tools is acculturative culture change. This culture change in the modern community suggests that Spier's inference of limited acculturation, while viable for the 19th century, is temporally limited and is best considered in a broader framework.

Bibliography

Chace, P. G.
    1976   Overseas Chinese Ceramics. In *The Changing Faces of Main Street*. R. S. Greenwood, ed. pp. 509-530. Ventura: City of San Buenventura Redevelopment Agency.

Elliott, W. W.
    1882   *History of Fresno County, California*. San Francisco: W. W. Elliott and Company.

Heizer, R. F. and A. J. Almquist
    1971   *The Other Californians*. Berkeley: University of California Press.

Herskovitz, M. J.
    1964   *Cultural Dynamics*. New York: A. A. Knopf.

Nordhoff, C.
    1874   *California: for Health, Pleasure and Residence*. New York: Harper and Brothers.

Langenwalter, P. E.
    1976   Interim Report on the Zooarchaeology of Four Miwok Sites along the Stanislaus River, Part 4. M. J. Moratto and L. M. Riley, eds. pp. 445-456. *Conservation Archaeology Papers*, No. 3. M. J. Moratto, gen. ed. San Francisco: San Francisco State University, Archaeological Research Laboratory.

Scheidt, W. A.
    1966   *A History of the Hidden Reservoir Area, Fresno River, California*. Report. Department of the Interior and U.S. Army Corps of Engineers, Sacramento District.

Simpson, G. G.
    1945   The Principles of Classification and a Classification of Mammals. *American Museum of Natural History, Bulletin 85*.

Spier, R. F. G.
    1958a Food Habits of Nineteenth-Century California Chinese. *California Historical Society, Quarterly* 37: 79-84, 129-136.
Spier, R. F. G.
    1958b Tool Acculturation Among 19th Century California Chinese. *Ethnohistory* 5: 97-117.
Switzer, R. R.
    1974 *The Bertrand Bottles*. A Study of 19th Century Glass and Ceramic Containers. U.S. Department of the Interior, National Park Service, Publications in Archaeology, No. 12.

CHAPTER 12

The Chinese on Main Street

ROBERTA S. GREENWOOD

If acquired solely through the traditional avenues of historical research, knowledge of the early Chinese community in Ventura, California, would be limited to the facts that it existed, and that its presence aroused hostility on the part of other settlers in this town which grew from and around Mission San Buenaventura. The existing accounts may be direct, such as the few articles on unique aspects like the Chinese Fire Company (Morrison 1958) or newspaper accounts of the celebrations of the Chinese New Year (Ventura Signal 1876: Jan. 29), activities of the Anti-Chinese League (Ventura Signal 1885: Jan. 8), or crimes committed in or ascribed to Chinatown. Other mentions may be indirect through passing reference in diaries, letters, or other publications. In fact, the first primary reference to the Chinese in Ventura is in a letter from pioneer settler Thomas Bard describing the presence of "Tartars" in the observance of July 4th, 1866 (Bard 1865-1869).

All of these descriptions derive, of course, from the Occidental hand or mind. Aside from reporting the presence of the Chinese, they are more useful as a reflection of the Anglo attitude than as description, interpretation, or explanation of Chinese culture. These accounts say nothing of the material culture, social organization, degree or process of acculturation except indirectly by implying the nature of the Anglo response which constituted some measure of the social parameter. Even the goods themselves, for the most part within 100 years old, have been unreported and unidentified. Books about Chinese ceramics have been oriented either to climax styles of archaeological periods and historical dynasties, or to ware manufactured specifically for export; in neither case do such studies illuminate the styles or technologies of the domestic or utilitarian items used by the workingclass Chinese.

The Ventura project was approached against the background of the history of the Chinese in California as related in such references as Chinese Historical Society (1969), Chiu (1967), Loosley (1927), Lyman (1970), Miller (1969), Sandmeyer (1939), and others. Immigration into California was prompted by a combination of the wars, famines, prestilences, and economic depression which afflicted China in the 1830s and 1840s, and stimulated by news of the Gold Rush in 1849. Initially, the Chinese were welcomed as laborers in the mines, but gold production from the surface placers decreased rapidly from the peak in 1852 (Clark 1970: 6) and the Chinese were subsequently displaced by mining laws. They were then employed in large numbers during the boom years of railroad construction but this, too, was a short-lived economic phenomenon.

The Chinese who worked at gold mining or on the railroad were mostly contract workers, rather than individual entrepreneurs, and their services were arranged and living conditions regulated by the supplier of labor. They lived in isolated camps, were communally fed, and typified the essential pattern of a male, frontier community with the extra dimensions of foreign origin and seasonal or project-related mobility. The Chinese immigrant of this period between 1850-1870 did not intend to establish permanent residence in California, but to accumulate his earnings and return to China. He thus lacked both the necessity to accommodate and the incentive to adapt to new lifeways. There are yet no archaeological data to test these assumptions, other than oral reports on surface observations (for example, Briggs 1978). Without context, there are no baselines for either the material goods representative of this early period or the cultural aspects of the isolated labor camps. Further, it may be questioned whether the usual standards of acculturation even apply when there is neither opportunity nor advantage to adapting to the host culture.

Gradually the Chinese moved into such occupations as food or laundry businesses, agriculture, merchandising, or domestic service, and the supposed competition for available employment led to the formation of the Anti-Chinese Union by organized labor in the 1870s, the Chinese Exclusion Act of 1882, the 1888 Scott Act, and the Geary Act of 1892. Although this was an urban rather than a frontier existence, the same assumption has been proposed but never tested: that acculturation was minimal. When the Mission Plaza Project began, it soon became apparent that documented history would yield little more than the facts that there were Chinese in Ventura by 1866 and that pressure was intense to disperse or demolish this settlement. Far from constituting an interpretive crutch, the written record was not even enough to lean on, and it was time to sharpen the archaeological tool kit (South 1974: 152).

The investigation was part of the environmental evaluation required when the Redevelopment Agency proposed a revitalization project on lands adjacent to Mission San Buenaventura. The full details and results of excavations in 1974 and 1975 have been published (Greenwood 1975, 1976). The first evidence of the Chinese presence on Main Street, perpendicular to Figueroa Street, included utilitarian ceramics, small glass medicinal vials, and opium pipe bowls found within the mix of aboriginal, Mission, and 19th century materials on a very disturbed site. Canton wares were factored out as exports related to the Mission years, as contrasted to the other goods used by the Chinese themselves. While suggestive, such items lacked social or chronological context. Eventually, two features were located which did provide assemblages which could be both tightly dated and associated to specific events in Ventura. These features, a well and a trash pit, have provided not only a data bank for the material goods included, but an inroad into the historic records of the period, illumination of a phase of the Chinese existence in this city which was totally unknown, some preliminary insights into the problems of dealing with such collections, and a number of inferences to be tested by future research into such deposits.

The goods recovered from the trash pit were approximately 75 per cent of Chinese origin, compared to 100 per cent western manufactures in comparably dated Anglo features (Benté 1976: 489). The non-Chinese goods in the well were predominantly glass beverage bottles and ceramic sherds; at least some of these, such as a Majolica fragment, may be attributed to mixture, disturbance, and the ultimate rapid filling of the well. An immediate difference was apparent between the vessel forms represented in the Chinese features and those recovered from Anglo trash pits and privies of comparable age on the same block (Table 1). While it may seem simplistic to point out that the non-Chinese households of whatever ethnic origin were setting their tables with the familiar place settings of plates and handled cups, and serving foods with platters and pitchers, the Chinese use of rice bowls and larger bowls indicates not only a difference in tableware but implies as well persistence of the traditional Oriental diet. The use of porcelain spoons and absence of European cutlery imply the continued use of chopsticks. The food jars are the brown stoneware containers in which staples were shipped from China, additional evidence for the diet. Faunal remains were predominantly pork and seafood. The assemblages within the two features do not reflect any changes in the degree of acculturation in the ten years between the deposition. Further, although the trash pit has been interpreted as the deposit of a family group probably living in the laundry which they operated and the well represents a one-time secondary deposition of trash of a communal nature from the lodgings within Chinatown, the distribution of food-related items within the two samples does not demonstrate any significant shifts other than the greater number of individuals and activities represented. There were differences: all of the Go counters, coins, and opium smoking accessories and more of the beverage bottles were recovered from the well, supporting the assumption that these reflected activities pursued in communal locations rather than in individual residences.

The questions of form and function may be addressed to the two features so close in time and space. The variability of goods in each is nil in those categories common to both, i.e., the same range, styles, and distribution of items. Variability in types, such as opium accessories or toys, leads to interpretive conclusions

Table 1. Summary of ceramic vessel forms in selected features

Chinese Features[a]	Well (ca. 1907) No.	%	Trash Pit (1890's) No.	%
Rice bowl	32	21	7	11
Soup/serving bowl	9	6	7	11
Tea cup	18	12	2	3
Wine cup	5	3	2	3
Dish	11	7	3	5
Spoon	13	9	3	5
Tea pot	3	2	2	3
Ginger jar	6	4	2	3
Wine bottle	20	13	9	14
Soy bottle	7	5	15	23
Food jars	25	17	10	16
Shallow pan	2	1	1	2
Lge. shipping jar	1	T	1	2
Total	152		64	

Non-Chinese Features[b]	Various No.	%
Cup/saucer	111	56
Plate	40	20
Bowl	9	5
Soup bowl	6	3
Platter	6	3
Lid	8	4
Pitcher	5	3
Oval boat	3	2
Tea pot	2	1
Chamber pot	7	4
Total	197	

[a] Chace 1976: 513-514
[b] Benté 1975: 226; 1976: 340.

of the demography involved. Such comparisons will reveal patterns of intrasite variability, while comparisons with contemporaneous non-Chinese features on the same block lead to analysis of the systemic structure of the broader society of Ventura. What was the basic function of the Chinatown, both to its own members and to the broader community, and was its status as an isolated sociocultural entity a deliberate action or a reaction to hostility? Are the assumptions advanced for the "frontier" labor camps typical of the Gold Rush or railroad construction applicable to the urban experience of the late 19th century?

The Chinese who first settled on Figueroa Street may have been some of those seeking a livelihood in Ventura after the collapse of employment opportunities in the mines or railroad camps, and their expectations in America may have been conditioned by this experience. Others may have been recent immigrants unexposed to any degree of culture contact. In either event, this settlement coincided with rising statewide pressures for Chinese exclusion. In Ventura, economic anxieties would have been exacerbated by the profound drought in the early 1860's which led to mass slaughter of cattle and economic depression. Although there has been no archaeological investigation of the first Chinatown on Figueroa Street, available records indicate that the very closely clustered settlement persisted despite openly expressed hostility.

By 1876, there were an estimated 200 Chinese within one block. By 1890, at least ten structures can be identified as Chinese, and on the Sanborn maps of 1892, eleven separate street addresses on the east side of the street and seventeen dwellings on the west side are labeled as Chinatown. The settlement remained intact in the face of both written and direct physical abuse until 1905-1906 when a drive for municipal modernization and development led to demolition of the white-owned buildings on Figueroa Street, and actual relocation of other structures around the corner to Main Street. The 1906 Sanborn map indicates only four Chinese-owned buildings left on the east side of Figueroa of the original Chinatown, and at least fourteen dwellings, some of them communal lodgings, and two laundries on Main Street, now labeled as Chinatown. The well and trash pit excavated were each behind one of these laundries.

It is not known whether the laundry operators were newly arrived or among those who were relocated within Ventura. Yet comparison of the goods from these features with inventories of comparable non-Chinese features on the same block and of the same age reveals that remarkably little acculturation had occurred in the 30-odd years of the Chinese experience in downtown Ventura. Certain of the most obvious distinctions are shown in Table 2; some of these distributions are mutually exclusive.

From the archaeological record, it is apparent that the greatest interaction with the host community is reflected in children's toys such as marbles, doll parts, toy dishes, and cast iron figures which were similar wherever they occurred. It is known that some Chinese children attended the local schools and such artifacts suggest a measure of acculturation. In other aspects of daily life, archaeological data support the proposition that even at this late date, adults maintained the traditional, homeland patterns in the choice, preparation, and service of food, use of opium and herbal medicinals, and native games. The seventy-five Chinese and Annamese coins from the well suggest an internal circulation within the enclave although other functions as gambling, talismanic, or ceremonial tokens are regarded as possible (Kleeb 1976: 497-508).

Table 2. Summary of traits in Chinese and non-Chinese features

	Chinese Features	Non-Chinese Features
Table wares	Porcelain spoons Porcelain cups Predominantly bowls	Metallic cutlery Glass tumblers Predominantly plates
Cooking	Iron pots Stoneware shipping jars Brass utensils related to wok Predominantly pork and seafoods	Enamelware utensils Glass canning jars Metallic cutlery Predominantly beef and sheep
Recreation	Opium smoking accessories Marbles, dolls, other toys Go counters, die, coins	Clay pipes Same Arms and ammunition
Medicinal	Glass vials and brass cans; herbal remedies	Glass bottles, patent and prescription remedies
Other	Shirt buttons only, attributed to laundries Wringer, sad irons, ink bottles, attributed to laundries Absent	Wide variety of buttons and clothing fasteners Occupational tools Chamber pots, cuspidors

Historical documents contribute another insight into the isolation of the Chinese settlement; although municipal sewers were installed along this block of Main Street in 1903, hook-ups to the adobes and wooden structures on the north side, constituting Chinatown, did not take place until 1925, when the Chinese quarter was no longer present. The implications are that the well was essential for both the lodgings and the laundry, and that the Chinese lacked basic public services available to others. Knowing this and the highly inflammable nature of their crowded occupation in the earlier Figueroa Street Chinatown, it is probable that the Chinese Fire Company of the 1870s was organized as a measure of self-defense. The brigade was in existence at least until 1905 but since its facility was on Figueroa, it may not have survived the move to Main Street.

Many implications for archaeology may be drawn from even this limited investigation. In contrast to the ceramics of the western world, it is easier to recognize the country of origin from even the smallest fragment of the Chinese wares, but infinitely harder to date them. It has become possible to recognize certain sequences in technology and style, such as the moulding of stoneware food jars or the shouldering on rice bowls, but as opposed to the well researched attributes of the export procelains, little is yet known about the manufacture of these utilitarian items except that change came slowly. Even the style or pattern names ascribed by American archaeologists are conveniently descriptive Western terminologies and not native names. Research is sorely needed in the country of origin, particularly in the province of Kwantung. As late as 1940, virtually all of the Chinese in this country, and their ceramics, had come from one of the seven districts whose major port is Canton (Light 1972: 81). Even when base marks are present, there are many problems in attempting to use them as the indicators so useful in identifying British or American ceramics (Evans 1978). The coins present another set of problems. Those found in Ventura included types dating back to 1662 for reasons peculiar to the Chinese monetary system, and their utility in site-dating should be approached with great caution. Lag dates between time of manufacture and discard may be less of a problem in Chinese deposits since both foods and beverages were imported in containers not subject to re-use; the stoneware vessels would be considered as expendable because the new supplies arrived in similar containers.

It should be apparent that many more descriptive reports will be required, from different types of sites and different periods, before specific models can be formulated for either the frontier or urban Chinese experience. It is essential that the data be recovered from tightly provenienced contexts before meaningful comparisons can be drawn. Although the goods are readily identifiable as Chinese, there is the danger of making ethnocentric cultural assumptions, such as the identification of a shallow cooking vessel by one investigator (mercifully, uncited) as a "milk pan."

In certain aspects, either the remote Chinese labor camp or the urban Chinatown of Ventura might be tested against the frontier model. In this sense, the site is considered as a nexus of socially integrating institutions within the larger, dispersed social entity (Lewis 1977: 172). Whether defined in a functional sense as a unit of organization (Arensberg 1961: 248), or in the spatial sense after Murdock (1949: 79), the Ventura Chinatown fits two of Lewis' three hypotheses advanced for Camden, extended to the urban setting. The enclave was in the primary center of trade, e.g., in the heart of downtown Ventura, which maximized contact and opportunity for interaction. The majority of the structures were associated with the centralizing functions such as business enterprises, social activities, or other collective purposes, rather than as individual dwellings alone. On the other hand, the Ventura Chinatown—like others—was not the typically dispersed settlement pattern on the frontier but was compact and tightly clustered like a market town. Presumably external sociocultural barriers to expansion were operating (Lewis 1977: 163), as well as aggregative forces from within. Chinatown was at the very least a frontier in the sense of an intrusive society in a new environment, confronted by both geographical and cultural boundaries, with trade networks and communication to the homeland while simultaneously performing a function in the host community. Other analogies in analysis and interpretation may be tested against the military models which reflect inventories of isolated male communities (South 1977a: 167-183), once archaeological inquiry is pursued into the mining or railroad labor camps.

In addition to supplying one of the first contextual assemblages of Chinese goods to be reported, the Ventura Mission Plaza project may help to illuminate the nature, causes, and processes of acculturation since this was only one of the many culture contacts which took place on the same block. In the lowest levels, there was apparently a period of abandonment rather than interaction between the aboriginal occupation dated at 3355 ± 70 B.P. (UGa-916) and the Chumash Indian village associated with the Mission founded in 1782. Archaeological data from these later years reveal how Tizon Brown ceramics were at first imported and finally manufactured by the neophytes, that the Indian community adopted new materials (making projectile points from bottle glass and Canton ceramics), new symbolism (crosses incised into steatite), and new forms (a handle on the traditional comal). More fundamental were the changes in Chumash social, religious, and economic life resulting from Missionization. By institutionalizing fishing to supplement the diet and procure goods for trade (Hudson 1976), the Mission deflated the status associated with one of the most cohesive elements in native society. Other rituals which also served to integrate Chumash society were subsumed into Catholic observances. Yet while it is the judgment of many scholars that the Indians did retain the basic values of their culture (Cook 1976: 157), the imposed and directed changes in subsistence, aggregation in unaccustomed groups, disruption of roles, spatial and social regulations so profoundly affected the culture that the Chumash were doomed before Secularization.

In contrast to the Chinese experience, the Mission assumed responsibility for the Indians, who responded in a number of ways: adapting some aspects of the new life, retaining some elements of their culture, and superficially accepting the directed changes. The white community of Ventura not only assumed no responsibility for the Chinese in their midst but denied them essential services, organized to tax and otherwise exclude them from Anglo society, and resorted to physical violence against both individuals and property. At least during the early years of residence, the Chinese never intended to adapt or integrate; since they planned to return to the homeland, there was no incentive to make accommodations beyond what was necessary to function economically. Since their attitude toward work was compatible with the values of the white community and they fulfilled agricultural, service, or other menial roles which were needed, most of the interaction was limited to the economic sphere. The Chinese culture thus remained essentially intact and it was Ventura which reacted—with hostility, fear, and overt actions which only served to reinforce the segregated settlement and the "foreign" ways.

Whereas the Indians were subject to control by the Mission, the Chinese were self-regulated: by their labor contracts in the early years of immigration, and by the Six Companies, surname associations, trade guilds and other special interest aggregations within Chinatown which governed business, welfare, and social institutions (Light 1972: 81-98). Instead of the directed cultural change imposed upon the Indians, the Chinese retained the option of rejecting acculturation, and their material culture as revealed archaeologically indicates maintenance of traditional customs. The Ventura evidence suggested that some measure of culture contact was taking place among children, but as late as 1950, institutionalized Chinese opium addicts were still isolated, alienated, single male sojourners. The decreased addiction after that date is regarded as a reflection of the long-delayed modernization of the Chinatown communities, gradual dissolution of the traditional subcultures, and perhaps more than anything, the severance of cultural ties with the homeland after the Communist ascendancy in mainland China in 1949 (Ball and Lau 1966: 71-72).

There was better reporting and fuller description of the Indians at the Mission than of the Chinese in Ventura some 100 years later. But then, the Indians were essential to the Mission's mission, while the exclusion of the Chinese was agitated by those whose skilled jobs and higher wage rates were actually in no way affected by Chinese competition. The drive for expulsion, bolstered by whatever degree of cultural and racial solidarity among the whites, was regarded as a cure-all for the various economic and social problems besetting California at the time (Chiu 1967: 138). Both the skimpy historical records and the survival of the culture should be examined against this background, and the most insightful approach to the lifeway may ultimately be provided through material goods revealed by the archaeological tool kit.

Acknowledgment

A portion of this work was made possible through the assistance of a research grant from the National Endowment for the Humanities. The findings and conclusions presented here do not necessarily represent the views of the Endowment.

Bibliography

Arensberg, Conrad M.
    1961   The community an object and sample. *American Anthropologist* 63: 241-264.
Ball, John C. and M. P. Lau
    1966   The Chinese narcotic addict in the United States. *Social Forces* 45: 68-72.
Bard, Thomas Robert
    1865- Unpublished letters. Ms. in Ventura County Library Historical Collec-
    1869   tion, Ventura, Ca.

Benté, Vance G.
- 1975 Trash pits, privies and promises. In, Greenwood 1975: 209-294.
- 1976 Good luck, long life. In, Greenwood 1976: 457-495. Well, a borrow pit and six privies. *Ibid.*, 299-350.

Briggs, Alton K.
- 1978 Chinese industrial nomads on the American frontier. Chinese railroad camps in Texas. Papers presented at the annual meeting of the Society for Historical Archaeology, Jan. 5, San Antonio.

Chace, Paul G.
- 1976 Overseas Chinese ceramics. In, Greenwood 1976: 509-530.

Chinn, Thomas W., ed.
- 1969 *A History of the Chinese in California.* Chinese Historical Society of America, San Francisco.

Chiu, Ping
- 1967 Chinese labor in California, 1850-1880, an economic study. Department of History, University of Wisconsin, Madison.

Clark, William B.
- 1970 Gold districts of California. *Bulletin 193, California Division of Mines and Geology.*

Cook, Sherburne F.
- 1976 *The conflict between the California Indian and white civilization.* University of California Press.

Evans, William S.
- 1978 Forms, fraud, fun and fundamentals: the marks on Chinese overseas ceramics. Paper presented at the annual meeting of the Society for Historical Archaeology, Jan. 5, San Antonio.

Greenwood, Roberta S., ed.
- 1975 *3500 years on one city block:* San Buenaventura Mission Plaza archaeological report. Redevelopment Agency, Ventura, Ca.
- 1976 *The changing faces of Main Street:* Ventura Mission Plaza archaeological project. Redevelopment Agency, Ventura, Ca.

Hudson, Dee Travis
- 1976 Chumash canoes of Mission Santa Barbara: the revolt of 1824. *Journal of California Anthropology* 3: 5-15.

Kleeb, Gerald N.
- 1976 Analysis of the coins from a Chinese trash pit in Ventura. In, Greenwood 1976: 497-508.

Lewis, Kenneth E.
- 1977 Sampling the archeological frontier: regional models and component analysis. In, South 1977b: 151-202.

Light, Ivan H.
- 1972 *Ethnic enterprise in America.* University of California Press.

Loosley, Allyn C.
- 1927 Foreign born population of California, 1848-1920. Unpublished thesis, University of California, Berkeley.

Lyman, Stanford M.
    1970   Strangers in the cities: the Chinese in the urban frontier. In, *Ethnic conflict in California,* ed. Charles Wollenberg, Tinnon-Brown, Inc., Santa Monica, 61-100.

Miller, Stuart C.
    1969   *The unwelcome immigrant: the American image of the Chinese, 1785-1882.* University of California Press.

Morrison, J. H.
    1958   San Buenaventura's Chinese fire company. *Ventura County Historical Society Quarterly* 3: 14-16.

Murdock, George Peter
    1949   *Social structure.* MacMillan, New York.

Sandmeyer, Elmer C.
    1939   *The anti-Chinese movement in California.* University of Illinois Press, Urbana.

South, Stanley
    1974   Palmetto Parapets. *Anthropological Studies 1.* University of South Carolina, Columbia.
    1977a *Method and theory in historical archeology.* Academic Press, New York.
    1977b *Research strategies in historical archeology.* Academic Press, New York.

Ventura Signal
    1876   April 15.
    1885   January 8.

CHAPTER 13
Archaeology of Asian American Culture: An Annotated Bibliography

ROBERT L. SCHUYLER

Because the number of references to Asian American archaeology is very limited a simple alphabetical arrangement by author has been adopted. All listings refer specifically to Asian Americans (Chinese) in North America and there is no attempt to cover the many citations of early Chinese trade pottery found on Euro-American sites. Sources taken from the *Newsletter* of the Society for Historical Archaeology (see under Schumacher, research compiler for the West Coast) are short current research announcements. In many cases they are, nevertheless, the only published source for a major project and are thus of critical importance for researchers.

Ayres, James E.
    1969 "Tucson's Chinese and Opium Smoking." Paper presented at the Second Annual Meeting of the Society for Historical Archaeology. Tucson, Arizona.
          "The Chinese in Tucson." Paper presented at the 1969 Annual Meeting of the Arizona Historical Convention. Tucson, Arizona.

    Two unpublished reports on the results of the Tucson Urban Renewal Project under the direction of James E. Ayres of the Arizona State Museum. Excavations in Chinese occupied areas have produced one of the richest collections from the Southwest.

Benté, Vance G.
    1976 Good Luck, Long Life. *The Changing Faces of Main Street*. Ed. Roberta Greenwood. San Buenaventura Mission Plaza Project Archaeological report Vol. 2: 457-495. Ventura, California.

Excavation of a wood-lined well and a domestic trash pit associated with a former Chinese laundry in Ventura has produced an impressive assemblage of ceramics, bottles, domestic glassware, toys, buttons, gaming pieces, opium smoking paraphernalia, cooking utensils and other items dating from the late 19th to the early 20th centuries. Artifacts are well described and quantified.

Briggs, Alton K.
1978 "Chinese Industrial Nomads on the American Frontier." "Chinese Railroad Camps in Texas." Papers presented at the Eleventh Annual Meeting of the Society for Historical Archaeology. San Antonio, Texas.

Important summaries of the excavation of railroad camp sites in West Texas. As these camps were located at the end of the construction sequence they produced impressive abandoned Chinese assemblages. Little evidence of acculturation.

Briggs, Alton K. and Paul G. Chace
1978 Historic Archaeology of Chinese Americans. Held at the Eleventh Annual Meeting of the Society for Historical Archaeology. San Antonio, Texas.

A special symposium organized by Briggs and Chace. For titles of individual presentations see under Briggs, Chace, Etter and Evans.

Chace, Paul G.
1966 Tung-Che Sites in California. *Archaeological Research Associates Bulletin* 11(2 & 3) p. 8. California State University, Long Beach.

1969 "Celestial Sojourners in the High Sierras; the Ethno-Archaeology of Chinese Railroad Workers (1865-1868)." Co-authored with William S. Evans, Jr. Paper presented at the Second Annual Meeting of the Society for Historical Archaeology. Tucson, Arizona.

Two reports of the survey and excavation of Chinese railroad camps near Donner Pass in the Sierra Nevada. Camps were small, all male occupied and most artifacts, except for bottle glass, were purely Chinese.

1976a Overseas Chinese Ceramics. *The Changing Faces of Main Street.* Ed. Roberta S. Greenwood. San Buenaventura Mission Plaza Project Archaeological Report Vol. 2: 509-530. Ventura, California.

A detailed descriptive catalogue of the Chinese ceramics from the Ventura project. Many whole or nearly whole vessels are illustrated along with sherds.

Chace, Paul G.
    1976b "Historic Chinese Porcelain and Stoneware in Indian Context." Paper presented at the 1976 Annual Meeting of the Society for California Archaeology. San Diego.

Unpublished report on the reuse of Chinese ceramics by Indians in several regions of the West.

    1978a "Overseas Chinese Ceramics in the Americas: the Historical Archaeology." Paper presented at the Eleventh Annual Meeting of the Society for Historical Archaeology. San Antonio, Texas.

General survey of collections from a wide range of rural and urban sites in Western America.

    1978b The Chinese in California. Held at the 1978 Annual Meeting of the Society for California Archaeology. Yosemite National Park, California.

Special symposium organized by Chace involving six presented papers. Those by Chace, Etter and one by Evans are repeats from the Texas meeting (see Briggs and Chace). For new papers see Evans and Krase.

Etter, Patricia A.
    1978 "The California Chinese and Opium Smoking." Paper presented at the Eleventh Annual Meeting of the Society for Historical Archaeology. San Antonio, Texas.

Inventory and description of opium-use related artifacts. (See Chapter 9 this volume).

Evans, William S.
    1978a "Overseas Chinese Material Culture in the West." Paper presented at the Eleventh Annual Meeting of the Society for Historical Archaeology. San Antonio, Texas.

General survey of the full range of Chinese material culture in the Western United States.

    1978b "Scrawls, Scribbles and Squibbles: Are the Marks on Chinese Pottery and Porcelain Meaningful?" "One Man's Archaeological Mark: the Chinese Cook at Rancho Los Cerritos." Papers presented at the 1978 Annual Meeting of the Society for California Archaeology, Yosemite National Park, California.

Evans, William S. and Paul G. Chace
 1978 "Forms, Fraud, Fun and Fundamentals: the Marks on Chinese Overseas Ceramics." Paper presented at the Eleventh Annual Meeting of the Society for Historical Archaeology. San Antonio, Texas.

Analysis of marks found on Chinese pottery. Symbolism as well as trademarks, manufacturer's marks and possible frauds are discussed.

Greenwood, Roberta S.
 1975 *3500 Years on One City Block.* San Buenaventura Mission Plaza Project Archaeological Report Vol. 1. City of San Buenaventura Redevelopment Agency. Ventura, California.

General monograph on the urban archaeology of Ventura with passing references to Asian American finds.

 1976 *The Changing Faces of Main Street.* San Buenaventura Mission Plaza Project Archaeological Report Vol. 2. City of San Buenaventura Redevelopment Agency. Ventura, California.

Most important published archaeological report on Asian American remains in California. See individual authors for chapters on local history (Wlodarski), archaeological features (Bente), coinage (Kleeb) and ceramics (Chace 1976a).

 1978 The Overseas Chinese at Home. *Archaeology* 31(5) 42-49.

A popular, well illustrated account of the Ventura excavations.

Kleeb, Gerald N.
 1976 Analysis of the Coins from a Chinese Trash Pit in Ventura. *The Changing Faces of Main Street.* Ed. Roberta S. Greenwood. San Buenaventura Mission Plaza Project Archaeological Report Vol. 2: 497-508. Ventura, California.

Analysis of 77 coins (3 Annamese, 62 genuine Chinese, 10 counterfeit Chinese and 2 United States) from one feature. An attempt to determine their use (for currency or ritual?) was not successful but did establish guidelines for future research.

Krase, Jean F.
 1978 "A Preliminary Analysis of English, Chinese, and Japanese Ceramics from the San Diego Presidio." Paper presented at the 1978 Annual Meeting of the Society for California Archaeology. Yosemite National Park, California.

Langenwalter, Paul E. II
  1977 The Archaeology of 19th Century Chinese Subsistence at Lower China Crossing, Madera County, California. Unpublished Ms. National Park Service, Interagency Archaeological Division, San Francisco.

  1978 "A Late 19th Century Chinese Store in the Sierran Foothills." Paper presented at the 1978 Annual Meeting of the Society for California Archaeology. Yosemite, California.

  See Chapter 10 in this volume.

Olsen, John
  1978 A Study of Chinese Ceramics Excavated in Tucson. *The Kiva* 44(1): 1-50. Arizona Archaeological and Historical Society. Tucson, Arizona.

  Archaeological investigations conducted in conjunction with the Tucson Urban Renewal Project by the Arizona State Museum have yielded one of the better Chinese American ceramic collections in the country. Detailed analysis of utilitarian wares by function, decoration and mode of manufacture provide one of the best published reference catalogues available.

Quellmalz, Carl Robert
  1972 Chinese Porcelain Excavated from North American Pacific Coast Sites. *Oriental Art* 18(2): 148-154.

Schumacher, Paul J. F.
  1971 Current Research: Pacific West — California. *Society for Historical Archaeology Newsletter* 3(4): p. 18.

  Passing mention of remains of Chinese in the Gold Mining Country, especially the Chinatown at Yreka.

  1972 Current Research: Pacific West — California. *Society for Historical Archaeology Newsletter* 5(3): 15-16.

  Survey in the New Melones Reservoir area, Calaveras County, located Chinese laborer's sites as well as unidentified structures from the Gold Rush period.

  1976a Current Research: Pacific West — California. *Society for Historical Archaeology Newsletter* 9(3): p. 27.

  Brief mention of the Ventura Chinatown project under Greenwood.

  1976b Current Research: Pacific West — California; — Nevada. *Society for Historical Archaeology Newsletter* 9(2): 25-26; 27.

First reference is to the Ventura Project. Second is concerned with the Nevada State Museum's test excavations of a major historic dump adjacent to the early Chinese settlement at Lovelock, Nevada. (MA Thesis on this material apparently being undertaken by Claudia Mazzeti at the University of Nevada.)

> 1976c Current Research: Pacific West – California. (Compiled by Barbara Gorrell for P. Schumacher.) *Society for Historical Archaeology Newsletter* 9(1): p. 53.

Paul Langenwalter's study of Chinese acculturation at Hidden Reservoir, Madera County is mentioned.

> 1977a Current Research: Pacific West – California. *Society for Historical Archaeology Newsletter* 10(2): 28-29.

Report of J. Michael Axford's discovery of 25 Chinese abalone processing camps on San Clemente Island dating from the late 19th century. Hearths, ceramics, opium boxes and iron cauldrons add a new dimension to Chinese activities on the coast of California. Mesa College project.

> 1977b Current Research: Pacific West – California. *Society for Historical Archaeology Newsletter* 10(1): p. 54.

Mention of work on Chinese settlement at the Harmony Borax Works in Death Valley. (See Teague and Shenk 1977).

> 1978 Current Research: Pacific West – California; – Nevada. *Society for Historical Archaeology Newsletter* 11(2): p. 3;43.

First report mentions Chinese materials excavated in the San Diego Gaslight district. Ceramics and glass opium lamps included. Second report concerns the excavation of trash pits and two wells at the small, rural Chinese settlement at Lovelock, Nevada (ca. 1885-1925).

Spier, Robert F. G.
> 1958 Tool Acculturation Among 19th Century California Chinese. *Ethnohistory* 5(2): 97-117.

A classic study of human behavior and material culture. Acculturation or resistence to acculturation depended on the degree of control by the dominant society and the presence or absence of analogs between Chinese and American industrial activities.

Teague, George A. and Lynette O. Shenk
> 1977 *Excavations at Harmony Borax Works.* Western Archaeological Center Publications in Anthropology No. 6. National Park Service, United States Department of the Interior. Washington, D.C.

General report on the survey and limited excavations at the Harmony Borax Works (1883-1888) in Death Valley National Monument. As the small labor force at the site was Chinese some interesting indications of acculturation were recovered from the adjacent townsite-Chinese quarters. Although ceramics were almost exclusively Chinese other artifact categories indicate more rapid acculturation of this all-male group than expected.

Tunnell, Curtis
    1971   Current Research: Gulf States — Texas. *Society for Historical Archaeology Newsletter* 4(2): 15-16.

Report of the field work by Alton Briggs at a Chinese laborer's camp of the Southern Pacific Rail Road in West Texas (1882-83). Stone tent outlines, double hearths and associated Chinese artifacts were recovered and mapped.

    1972   Current Research: Gulf States — Texas. *Society for Historical Archaeology Newsletter* 5(2): p. 10.

Passing reference to the remains of "Chinese import shops" in a general urban excavation in downtown El Paso.

Wlordarski, Robert J.
    1976   A Brief History of Chinatown in Ventura. *The Changing Faces of Main Street.* Ed. Roberta S. Greenwood. San Buenaventura Mission Plaza Project Archaeological Report Vol. 2: 440-456. Ventura, California.

A historical summary of a typical, small Chinatown that existed in Ventura from the 1860's to the 1920's. Scene of archaeological investigations under Greenwood from 1974 to 1976.

Wood, Donald G.
    1970   "Chinese Porcelain Types as Expressed at Yreka Chinatown." Paper presented at the 1970 Annual Meeting of the Society for California Archaeology. Asilomar, California.

Unpublished presentation of materials recovered from an abandoned Chinatown (ca. 1878-1940) in Northern California.

PART THREE
Archaeology and Ethnicity

CHAPTER 14

Approaches to Ethnic Identification in Historical Archaeology

MARSHA C.S. KELLY
ROGER E. KELLY

The issue to which we address ourselves is that of ethnic identification, from both the cultural anthropological and archaeological points of view. Cultural anthropologists have been becoming increasingly aware of the complexities of dealing with ethnic identity, especially over the last decade or so. From their research, we feel that there are some aspects relating to this complexity which need to be discussed at present, so that archaeologists, particularly historical archaeologists, may be made more aware and less accepting of seemingly clearcut ethnic identification. Even with the utilization of ethnographic and historic sources, ethnic identification of a site may not be facile.*

Current concepts from cultural anthropology need to be brought to the consideration of historical archaeologists to indicate the difficulties in dealing with ethnic identification. We think that Kushner states the problem very well when he says "... what is identity but another referent for the host of questions, dilemmas, and paradoxes with which we are engaged when we speak of culture" (Kushner 1974: 126). This comment indicates the can of worms that one opens when trying to identify an ethnic group. If this is true for the cultural anthropologist, who generally has living informants, it must be equally true for the historical archaeologist who has to rely on data from historical records and data from the ground which archaeological investigations produce. Sol Tax observed, as far back as 1960, that outward cultural forms of a culture may change while the "subtler or inner aspects of culture" and their meanings may still remain the same over very extended periods of time (Tax 1960: 194).

A growing cognizance of the problem of ethnic identification, on the part of cultural anthropologists, is demonstrated by an increasing number of differing and varied theoretical approaches to the issue. The approaches seem to divide themselves into two general categories: first, broad theories which attempt to deal with the problem as a whole; and second, narrower or more specific theoretical approaches which attempt to deal only with parts of the problem of identifying ethnic groups. Since time does not permit great detail, we will mention only three or four examples.

In the category of over-all theories, perhaps one of the earliest known is that which Fredrik Barth put forward in 1969. He says that the persistence of ethnic group identity depends on the maintenance of a social boundary. Such boundaries, states Barth, may have territorial counterparts but are primarily characterized by three aspects of social behavior. These aspects are the following (Barth 1969: 15):

1. criteria for determining membership and ways of signalling membership and exclusion;
2. complex organization of behavior and social relations which implies a sharing of criteria for evaluation and judgment;
3. situations of social contact between persons of different cultures and ... a structuring of interaction which allows the persistence of cultural differences.

Such differences exist despite the movement of people across them. Hence, ethnic distinctions do not depend on lack of mobility, contact or information, but rather on stable social relations which are maintained on the basis of dichotomized ethnicity; that is, a dichotomy between "we," the people, and everyone else in the world who are "others."

This dichotomy between the internal identification of a group by its own members and the external identification of that group by non-members is perhaps the most basic of the complexities involved in dealing with ethnic identification, and affects both the research of the cultural anthropologist and the archaeologist. One way of looking at this dichotomy has been suggested by Spicer (1971: 798). Instead of attempting to discern traits of material culture, such as house types, to identify an ethnic group, Spicer has suggested that we look for symbols by which any group may identify itself or use as a contrast to outwardly imposed identity. Such symbols may reflect material culture, such as a flag, or non-material culture, such as a language. Such symbols may change or be replaced, totally or in large part, and yet the group identity still be strongly maintained (Spicer 1975: 41). One can readily envision the problems which such replacement poses for the cultural anthropologist. How much more difficult it makes things for the archaeologist who usually cannot probe living informants and should, therefore, be on guard against making a seemingly obvious ethnic identification from written sources and field research. Spicer conveys to his readers that ethnic self-identification is a hardy thing and that we should respect its tenacity!

Another general theoretical approach to the problem of identify is to view ethnic groups as categories of ascription; that is the group is a category to the extent that it is so defined by others. Authors who have worked with this concept include Knutsson (1969) and De Vos (1975). De Vos and Romanucci-Ross have noted that, "... the external force of ascription exercised by ..." other societies is as strong as self-identification (De Vos and Romanucci-Ross 1975: 378).

In contrast to the general approaches mentioned above, there are also many approaches to the study of specific aspects of ethnic identification or "ethnicity," which is a term growing in popularity. Anthropologists are beginning to look at the effects of migration on ethnic identity (Du Toit and Safa 1975). Certainly, examples such as Jewish and Basque migrations and that of a small group of southwestern Native Americans show the relationship between migration and ethnic identity to be a fascinating one, and one which needs much further exploration.

Other research is examining ways in which ethnicity is generated, transmitted, and changed (Epstein 1978). These issues may not sound overly specific, but compared with giving attention to the issue of ethnicity as a whole, they are. This variety of approaches, which is becoming more prevalent in the literature, appears to indicate an increased awareness of and interest in the complexity of the concept on the part of cultural anthropologists. We wish to suggest that archaeologists should anticipate dilemmas concerning ethnic identification similar to or perhaps more difficult than those faced by cultural anthropologists. This is particularly true in acculturation situations such as the Black and Chinese contact sites described in this volume.

In terms of cultural anthropology, a brief example will highlight the difficulties which hasty decisions regarding ethnicity can produce. The ethnic group which the senior author studied was originally composed of four ethnic groups who migrated to what is now south central Arizona from the present California side of the Colorado River at differing times during the first half of the 19th century. The name Maricopa was imposed on all such groups, who lived in close proximity to each other, by Anglos. In 1963, one of these peoples, the Halchidoma, was reported as no longer having an identity separate and distinct from that of the Maricopa. This decision on the part of the Anglo investigators was based on the fact that the " 'specific pattern assemblage' of traits comprising" the culture of this sub-group, if you wish, no longer existed (Dobyns, Ezell and Ezell 1963: 137). The statement regarding material culture is quite true. Yet, the fact remained, in the early 1970's, that there were still people who identified themselves and were identified by others as being Halchidoma (Kelly 1972). Thus, in this case, reliance on written records and field observation of the obvious was misleading. Identity is very complex.

When one thinks of the ethnic group and reservation studied in terms of data which will be available to future archaeologists, many pitfalls are evident in appreciating the identities of the people who live there, especially if there were no aid in the form of written records. Material culture is almost exclusively

Anglo, except for some houses which are Pima in type (Pimas being the other, and numerically dominant, ethnic group on the reservation). The distinctive pottery which the Maricopas make is made to be sold as a source of income. Thus not much of it will be found in future archaeological remains of Maricopa houses.

Even with the help of ethnographic resources, the bulk of which date to the 1930's (Spier 1933), it is not likely that an archaeologist excavating 1970's Marciopa culture would have any appreciation for the strength of their identity at that point in time. Acculturation would probably be the most obvious assumption as to what happened to the ethnic identity of the Maricopa. This is not to say that there has not been considerable acculturation or more correctly, in the case of the Maricopa, what Spicer calls 'selective borrowing' (Spicer 1975). However, despite selective borrowing, particularly as regards material culture, Maricopa identity is vital and intact in the 1970's. This example would be an archaeological counterpart to the earlier discussion of the Halchidoma. In both instances, ethnic affiliation could be incorrect, which only indicates that both ethnographers *and* archaeologists must be cautious in the use of documentary evidence.

Along these lines, a colleague of ours has suggested another situation which illustrates difficulties an historical archaeologist might face regarding ethnic identification. How would one distinguish a "Spanish-American sheepherder's camp from a Navajo summer camp from an oil driller's camp, all comtemporaneous and even within the same section? There would be differences in material culture, which one could expect. But what if basic equipment and foodstuffs were furnished to all three by an Anglo employer? The camp remains would be virtually indistinguishable without informant data" (Wilson, personal communication).

A tantalizing suggestion that historical archaeologists are becoming aware of, and beginning to deal with, the complexities of ethnicity occurs in the chapter by Vernon Baker concerning an early 19th century house known to have belonged to a freed Black woman. He has attempted to discern cultural patterns which are not clearly distinguishable as either Anglo or Black. The possibilities of this and other such approaches to ethnic identification of an historic site are encouraging, and demonstrate that archaeologists are becoming aware of the need for caution.

Recognizing then, that ethnic identification and "ethnicity" are current interests of cultural anthropologists and some historical archaeologists, how can these interests flourish in historic sites research? There seem to us to be four principle reasons for addressing ethnic identification questions; these are the following (no priority intended):

1. *Research design endeavors* in site specific, area, or regional applications. The ethnic homogeneity or heterogeneity of a defined space ought to be

as important as whether historic sites are present or not (see King, Hickman, and Berg 1978, House 1978, Lewis 1978).

This first point will be elaborated upon in a moment but the remaining three points will be mentioned only briefly.

2. Ethnic identification via archaeological techniques in *planning* and *resource management plans* should not be forgotten. Historic park research especially requires attention to ethnic identification. In California, new state historic parks will include a 19th century mining town, a Black cooperative community, a Chinese shrimp camp, and a detention camp for Japanese citizens held during World War II. Completed management plans for Bodie, California—the mining town—include recognition of Chinese and Native American resident populations (Felton and others 1977). Ethnic significance can be critical in compliance. Ethnic identification should also be part and parcel of *fabric restoration/stabilization projects* on historic structures, especially when a multi-ethnic occupancy is suspected (Teague and Shenk 1977).

3. We wish to emphasize again the point made by Flemming (1971) several years ago concerning the value of the *"consciousness-raising" theme* in historical archaeological projects. Recent projects at Parting Ways, Sandy Ground, and Boston's Beacon Hill should alert historical archaeologists to continued *public education values*. The Urban Park and Recreation Recovery Act of 1978 may provide opportunities for other historical archaeological education programs.

4. As a companion to other disciplines, *ethnic identification* studies in historical archaeology have *significant roles* in *sister disciplines* within anthropology, as noted, and in history, economics, sociology, and even landscape architecture. One recent example is the study of the waterfront of Newburyport, Massachusetts which had an historical land use theme as well as archaeological interests (Faulkner and others 1978).

Returning to the first point, that of the role of ethnic identification questions in research designs, we want to point out the relationships of ethnic identification questions to a) documents, b) material culture, c) actions and patterns in the archaeological record, and finally, d) ethnic identification as reality.

Documents

Because historical archaeology is aided by texts of all sorts—living (informants) and static (written materials)—it has a special direction and responsibility. We all know that major documents and those "small documents forgotten" such as coin inscriptions, trademarks or labels or even grafitti usually speak to the "ideal" past culture, not the "real" cultural situation (Kutsche, van Ness, and Smith 1976: 13), Schuyler 1977). The relationship of what is said in documents or by informants and what may be in the ground is a testable situation, not a facile situation. This is part of the "artifact-document" nexus which Schuyler (1978: 252) says must be recognized if historical archaeology is to make its own contributions. Ethnic identification questions taken from documentary sources may be correct, but will doubtless be incomplete unless some of the concepts and tools from cultural anthropological colleagues are transformed into testable statements. Although Glassie (1977: 30) warns, "hypotheses too rapidly and trimly formed will nearly guarantee triviality," we should attempt to examine even the obviously clear ethnic affiliation of a site's occupants since complete reliance on historical documentation is not always adequate. What then are those specific items of artifact assemblages or material culture sets which could be isolated from documents and tested, whether we are using techniques of historiography or ethnoarchaeology? Can we speak of the symbolic or boundary maintenance value to those items in a manner compatible with Spicer or Barth?

Material Culture

We all know that assemblages of material culture can be misleading, ambiguous, or erroneous when used for ethnic identification questions but we continue to use gun flints, tea sets, ceramics or coins, or opium equipment because they have lasted and the people have not (Glassie 1977: 28). Several writers have warned us about the icon-like nature of tin cans (Ascher 1974: 12), or soft-drink bottles (Gilborn 1970) or other "unrespectable" items (Fontana 1968) or folk-artifacts as encapsulated survivals of earlier lifestyles (Glassie 1977). We think that the categorization of material culture from archaeological research along the lines of Human Relations Area Files (HRAF) will yield more sensitive classes of items reflective than any other customary format of provenience, function, or substance. We note that Cotter (1968) and South (1977) and others use HRAF formats. We offer two statements relative to ethnic identification from material culture, recognizing inherent problems:

1. In any HRAF category, those items of local origin will be better indicators of ethnic identification than those of greater distance, with the exception of intrusive items having high symbolic value.
2. Those elements of material culture which are shown to have primary roles in facilitating social persistence or adaptation will be more sensitive to ethnic identification purposes than other categories such as survival, recreation/entertainment, and so forth.

Actions and Patterns

We are not alone in recognizing that South's "patterns" and Shiffer's (1977) "behavior patterns" could be combined into useful tools. If South is correct in saying "the first responsibility of the archaeologist is pattern recognition," then the second responsibility is to contrast the perceived pattern with others, using behavior pattern analyses. Edward Spicer has demonstrated that "opposition" of ethnic groups' patterns is one means of continuing each group's persistence as an entity (1971). Why not see if the Carolina, Frontier or Brunswick Patterns proposed by South (1977) are actually means by which each community attempted to emphasize cultural difference even though each pattern was a geographical variation of one broad cultural tradition? Would analyses of Parting Ways, Sandy Ground, Weeksville, Skunk Hollow, Beacon Hill or even Allensworth, California patterns show contrastive behavior patterns which are not defined by the caste lines of slavery or racial discrimination? Baker's analysis of Black Lucy's garden seems to be along these lines. Would the Bodie, California pattern be successfully compared with the Silcott, Washington pattern as "Anglo" settlements (Adams 1976)? What about the contrastive Chinese behavior patterns in Ventura, California (Greenwood 1978) and those in Bodie or in all-male Chinese behavior patterns along railroad construction camps or near a borax processing plant (Teague and Shenk 1977)? We would like to see testable statements about "opposition" between ethnic groups and their respective mileux as one way to arrive at law-like statements relative to the archaeological study of ethnic lifeways and their persistence. We also note that artifact-free space *may* be tangible evidence of social boundaries at work and therefore may be as much a product of pattern behavior as an artifact scatter pattern (Binford 1978).

Ethnic Identification As Reality

Together with our prehistorian colleagues who sometimes attempt to apply social models to archaeological interpretation (for example, see Rock 1974), we too face troublesome problems in applying current ideas to past data. Problems include the following:

1. Atypical group occupancy, such as all male or female, one age group, migratory populations, seasonality, or other imbalances. But as the Maricopa/Halchidoma data and Harmony Borax data indicate, ethnic persistence and our identification of it are possible even though an occupancy was unusual in some way. Still, we will not be able to observe this without sensitive research designs (Kelly and Ward 1972).

2. Ideosyncratic or highly personalized behavior may still be useful in addressing ethnic patterns (Hickman 1977) but caution should be the byword.
3. Several historical archaeologists have recently noted the value of class or status research questions (Carrillo 1977, Otto 1977) but here may be a blurring of ethnic identification by a "culture of poverty" which may cut across groups. Would ethnic identification still be possible? We are not sure.
4. The sparseness of the archaeological record may defeat us if site integrity or complexity has been compromised. At least, a researcher should note this less-than-minimal condition as preventing the type of research we have been discussing. Many historic sites will likely fall into this realistic category but may have other contributions to make.

It has been about ten years since Cleland and Fitting (1968) discussed the crisis in identity of historical archaeology. We think that many of the chapters in this volume and papers read at recent scholarly meetings indicate that a "more thoughtful orientation" to historical archaeology which Cleland and Fitting desired has developed in time to defuse the crisis. Ethnic identification can be another positive force and effective conceptual tool, in part borrowed from our anthropological colleagues.

Acknowledgments

We are appreciative of personal communications and suggestions from John P. Wilson, archaeological and historical research consultant, Las Cruces, New Mexico and to Robert L. Schuyler for his editorial comments.

Bibliography

Adams, William H.
   1976 *Silcott, Washington: Ethnoarcheology of a Rural American Community*. Ph.D. dissertation, Department of Anthropology, Washington State University Pullman.
Ascher, Robert
   1974 Tin*Can Archaeology. *Historical Archeology*. Vol. 8, pp. 7-16. Athens.
Barth, Fredrik
   1969 Introduction. In *Ethnic Groups and Boundaries*, edited by Fredrik Barth, pp. 9-38. Little, Brown and Company, Boston.
Binford, Lewis R.
   1978 Dimensional Analysis of Behavior and Site Structure: Learning from an Eskimo Hunting Stand. *American Antiquity* 43: 330-361.

Carrillo, Richard F.
  1977 Archeological Variabilility—Sociocultural Variability. In *Research Strategies in Historical Archeology*, edited by Stanley South, pp. 73-89. Academic Press.
Cotter, John
  1968 *Handbook for Historical Archeology. Part 1.* privately printed. Wyncote, Pa.
Cleland, Charles E. and James E. Fitting
  1968 The Crisis of Identity: Theory in Historic Sites Archeology. In *The Conference on Historic Site Archaeology Papers*, pp. 124-138, edited by Stanley South. University of South Carolina, Columbia.
Deetz, James
  1977 Material Culture and Archeology—What's the Difference. In *Historical Archeology and the Importance of Material Things.* pp. 9-12, edited by Leland Ferguson. Special Publication No. 2. Society for Historical Archeology.
DeVos, George
  1975 Ethnic Pluralism: Conflict and Accommodation. In *Ethnic Identity: Cultural Continuities and Change*, pp. 5-41, edited by George De Vos and Lola Romanucci-Ross. Mayfield Publishing Company, Palo Alto.
DeVos, George and Lola Romanucci-Ross, editors
  1975 *Ethnic Identity: Cultural Continuities and Change.* Mayfield Publishing Company, Palo Alto.
Dobyns, Henry F., Paul H. Ezell and Greta S. Ezell
  1963 Death of a Society. *Ethnohistory* 10: 105-161.
Du Toit, Brian M. and Helen I. Safa, editors
  1975 *Migration and Development: Implications for Ethnic Identity and Political Conflict.* Beresford Book Service, Chicago.
Epstein, A. L.
  1978 *Ethos and Identity: Three Studies in Ethnicity.* Beresford Book Service, Chicago.
Faulkner, Alaric, Kim Mark Peters, David P. Sell, and Edwin S. Dethlefsen
  1978 *Port and Market: Archaeology of the Central Waterfront, Newburyport, Massachusetts.* Report submitted to Interagency Archeological Service, Atlanta, Heritage Conservation and Recreation Service, Department of the Interior.
Felton, David L., Francis Lortie, Kathleen Davis, and Leslie Davis
  1977 *The Cultural Resources of Bodie State Historic Park.* Resource Preservation and Interpretation Division, Cultural Heritage Section, Department of Parks and Recreation, State of California. Sacramento.
Flemming, Ronald Lee
  1971 After the Report, What?; The Uses of Historical Archaeology, a Planner's View. *Historical Archeology*, Vol. 5, pp. 49-61.
Fontana, Bernard L.
  1968 Bottles, Buckets, and Horseshoes: The Unrespectable in American Archaeology. *Keystone Folklore Quarterly*, 13: 171-184.

Gilborn, Craig
   1970   Pop Iconology: Looking at the Coke Bottle. In *Icons of Popular Culture*, pp. 13-28, edited by Marshall Fishwick and Ray B. Browne, Bowling Green.

Glassie, Henry
   1977   Archeology and Folklore: Common Anxieties, Common Hopes. In *Historical Archaeology and the Importance of Material Things*, pp. 23-25, edited by Leland Ferguson, Special Publication No. 2, Society for Historical Archeology.

Greenwood, Roberta S.
   1978   The Overseas Chinese at Home: Life in a Nineteenth Century Chinatown in California. *Archeology*, 31: 4, 42-49.

Hickman, Patricia Parker
   1977   Country Nodes: An Anthropological Evaluation of William Keys' Desert Queen Ranch, Joshua Tree National Monument, California. *Publications in Anthropology*, No. 7, Western Archeological Center, National Park Service, Tucson.

House, John H.
   1977   Survey Data and Regional Models in Historical Archeology. In *Research Strategies in Historical Archeology*, pp. 241-260, edited by Stanley South, Academic Press.

Kelly, Marsha C. S.
   1972   The Society that Did Not Die. *Ethnohistory*, 19: 261-265.

Kelly, Roger E. and Albert Ward
   1972   Lessons from the Zeyouma Trading Post near Flagstaff, Arizona. *Historical Archeology*, Vol. 6, pp. 65-76.

King, Thomas F., Patricia Parker Hickman, and Gary Berg
   1977   *Anthropology in Historic Preservation: Caring for Culture's Clutter*. Academic Press.

Knutsson, Karl Eric
   1969   Dichotomy and Integration. In *Ethnic Groups and Boundaries*, pp. 86-110, edited by Fredrik Barth. Little, Brown and Company, Boston.

Kushner, Gilbert
   1974   Discussion. In *Social and Cultural Identity; Problems of Persistence and Change*, pp. 126-133, edited by Thomas K. Fitzgerald, Southern Anthropological Society Proceedings, No. 8. University of Georgia, Athens.

Kutsche, Paul, John R. Van Ness, and Andrew T. Smith
   1976   A Unified Approach to the Anthropology of Hispanic Northern New Mexico: Historical Archeology, Ethnohistory, and Ethnography. *Historical Archeology*, Vol. 10, pp. 1-16.

Lewis, Kenneth E.
   1977   Sampling the Archeological Frontier: Regional Models and Component Analysis. In *Research Strategies in Historical Archeology*, pp. 151-201, edited by Stanley South. Academic Press.

Otto, John S.
   1977   Artifacts and Status Differences—A Comparison of Ceramics from Planter, Overseer, and Slave Sites on an Antebellum Plantation. In *Research Strategies in Historical Archeology,* pp. 91-118, edited by Stanley South. Academic Press.

Rock, James T.
   1974   The Use of Social Models in Archaeological Interpretaion. *The Kiva,* 40: 1-2; 81-91, Tucson.

Schiffer, Michael B.
   1977   Toward a Unified Science of the Cultural Past. In *Research Strategies in Historical Archeology,* pp. 13-40, edited by Stanley South. Academic Press.

Schuyler, Robert L.
   1977   The Spoken Word, the Written Word, Observed Behavior and Preserved Behavior: The Contexts Available to the Archeologist. In *The Conference on Historic Site Archaeology Papers,* pp. 99-120, edited by Stanley South, University of South Carolina, Columbia.
   1978   Future Trends. In *Historical Archaeology: A Guide to Substantive and Theoretical Contributions,* pp. 251-252, edited by R. L. Schuyler. Baywood Publishing Company, Farmingdale, New York.

South, Stanley, editor
   1977   *Method and Theory in Historical Archeology.* Academic Press.
   1978   Pattern Recognition in Historical Archaeology. *American Antiquity,* 43; 2; 223-30.

Spicer, Edward H.
   1971   Persistent Cultural Systems. *Science,* 174: 795-800.
   1975   Indian Identity versus Assimilation. In *An Occasional Paper of the Weatherhead Foundation,* pp. 31-54. The Weatherhead Foundation, New York.

Spier, Leslie
   1963   *Yuman Tribes of the Gila River.* The University of Chicago Press.

Tax, Sol
   1960   Acculturation. In *Men and Cultures; Selected Papers of the Fifth International Congress of Anthropological and Ethnological Sciences,* edited by Anthony F. C. Wallace. University of Pennsylvania Press.

Teague, George A. and Lynette O. Shenk
   1977   Excavations at Harmony Borax Works: Historical Archeology at Death Valley National Monument. *Publications in Anthropology,* No. 6, Western Archeological Center, National Park Service, Tucson.

Contributors

VERNON G. BAKER is a Research Associate of the Robert S. Peabody Foundation for Archaeology. He has taught at the University of Massachusetts and MIT and is completing his doctoral dissertation in Anthropology at Brown University. Among his several publications on New England historical archaeology is a monograph on *Historical Archaeology at Black Lucy's Garden*.

BETH ANNE BOWER is Staff Archaeologist for the Museum of Afro-American History in Boston. She has studied historical archaeology at Brown University, from which she holds the M.A. degree, and is at present a Ph.D. candidate in the Department of American Civilization at Boston University.

SARAH BRIDGES is Archaeologist for the National Register of Historic Places, Washington, D.C. She is in the Ph.D. Program at New York University from which she received the M.A. Her primary interest is the historical archaeology of the Northeast, particularly the contact period.

PATRICIA A. ETTER is finishing her B.A. in Anthropology at the California State University in Long Beach where she also expects to do graduate work. She is a long time resident of California and is currently doing research on the ethnohistory of the state.

WILLIAM S. EVANS, JR. is a Professor of Anthropology at Santa Monica College in California. He has been involved in several archaeological projects in Southern California that investigated the different ethnic groups that entered the state during the historic period.

LELAND G. FERGUSON is Visiting Assistant Professor of Anthropology at the University of South Carolina. He is currently conducting research on material remains of the proto-historic and early historic period of the Southeast.

JOAN H. GEISMAR received her B.A. from Barnard College and is currently a doctoral student in Anthropology at Columbia where she received her M.A.

degree. Skunk Hollow is her dissertation topic. Interests include Afro-American archaeology and the prehistory of the Northeast, particularly as it pertains to the New York–New Jersey area.

ROBERTA S. GREENWOOD is Research Associate at the Natural History Museum of Los Angeles County, and Principal Investigator of Greenwood and Associates, consultants in cultural resource management. Among her recent projects are the multiple historic sites within the Dry Creek-Warm Springs Valleys Archaeological District, a Corps of Engineers dam in California.

GEOFFREY M. GYRISCO received his B.A. in history from Cornell in 1975 and is currently working on his Ph.D. in American Civilization at George Washington University. His areas of specialization are historical archaeology and historic preservation. Since 1977 he has held a part-time student appointment at Interagency Archaeological Services of the Heritage Conservation and Recreation Service, U.S. Department of the Interior.

MARSHA C. S. KELLY is a cultural anthropologist with interests in Native American ethnography and identity, material culture of 19th-20th century America, and cultural events as identity maintenance. She has published in several journals and has an article on the Maricopa in the Southwest volume of the *Handbook of North American Indians*. She is finishing her Ph.D. dissertation at the University of Arizona.

ROGER E. KELLY is Regional Archaeologist, Western Region, National Park Service, San Francisco. He received his Ph.D. in Anthropology from the University of Arizona in 1971 and has taught at Tucson, Northern Arizona University, and California State University at Northridge. His interests include historic site archaeology, cultural resource management policy implementation, and archaeological theory.

PAUL E. LANGENWALTER II is a Research Associate at the Natural History Museum of Los Angeles County in the Archaeology and Vertebrate Paleontology Sections. He is a graduate student at the University of California-Riverside and is presently studying historic and prehistoric California subsistence patterns.

JOHN SOLOMON OTTO received his Ph.D. from the University of Florida and is currently Visiting Assistant Professor at Brown University. His interest in plantation archaeology has recently been expanded to the study of slaveholding farms in western Arkansas.

BYRON RUSHING is President of the Museum of Afro-American History in Boston. Although he has studied the Black history of that city he is concerned with the history of all Afro-American communities in New England.

BERT SALWEN is Professor of Anthropology at New York University and Archaeologist (part-time) for policy planning and education at the Interagency Archaeological Services in Washington, D.C. He is a leading expert on the prehistoric, historic and ethnohistoric periods of northeastern North America. He has published widely on these topics and recently co-edited *Amerinds and Their Paleoenvironments in Northeastern North America*.

ROBERT L. SCHUYLER is Associate Curator in Charge of the American Historical Archaeology Section of the University Museum, University of Pennsylvania. As Associate Professor he also teaches in the Departments of American Civilization and Anthropology. He received his B.A. from the University of Arizona and his M.A. and Ph.D. from UC-Santa Barbara. His interests include the full range of historical archaeology from contact sites to the industrial period. He recently published *Historical Archaeology, A Guide to Substantive and Theoretical Contributions* and is editor of the new journal *North American Archaeologist.*